MW00748213

gone

By Best-Selling Author
DIANNE WILSON

going
going
gone

THE MOMENT OF SURRENDER

By Best-Selling Author
DIANNE WILSON

GONE Published by Dianne Wilson

First published in the USA in 2013

Copyright © Dianne Wilson 2013

ISBN 978-0-9840387-4-9

Photography of Dianne Wilson: Natalie Chenier

www.natalielynnphotography.com

Cover Graphics: Corey Meyers

Typeset in Newport Beach California.

Printed in the USA.

Author Contact Details:

Dianne Wilson

Newport Church PO Box 9577

Newport Beach, CA 92658 USA

Email: dianne.wilson@newportchurch.com

Tel: +1.949.673.1136

Dear Heavenly Father,

Thank you for the privilege of knowing Jesus and making Him known.

Amen.

the author

Dianne is a bestselling author [published by both HarperCollins Australia and Random House Australia] and spokesperson on the issues of body, soul, spirit, healthy living, healthy body image, value and identity. Dianne and her husband Jonathan are the Senior Pastors of Newport Church in Orange County, California. Dianne's entrepreneurial approach to life, and her passionate message of freedom have created a platform for her to help many people. Dianne has devoted her life to seeing people live in freedom and released into all that they were created to be. Born and raised in Sydney, Australia, wife of an amazing husband, mother of many gorgeous children, and grandmother too, Dianne is a passionate church builder – loving God, loving people and loving life! Founding Director of the Imagine Foundation, Dianne has a dream of placing a copy of her book Mirror Mirror in the hands of every 9th Grade school girl across the USA.

Other Books by Dianne Wilson:

★   It's Time – *leadership & character development*
★   Body & Soul – *a body & soul shaping handbook*
★   Here To Eternity – *a book of hope in seasons of loss*
★   Mirror Mirror [English and Spanish] – *an identity & self-esteem handbook*
★   Fat Free Forever! – *a body shaping handbook*
★   Back in Shape After Baby – *a body shaping handbook*
★   Fat Free Forever Cookbook – *a body shaping cookbook*
★   Fat Free Forever 101 Tips – *a body shaping minibook*
★   Easy Exercise for Everybody – *an body shaping handbook*

Lifestyle Courses by Dianne Wilson:

★   Mirror Mirror – *a body & soul lifestyle course*
★   Body & Soul – *an identity & self-esteem course*

"Her heart is full of another world,
even when her hands are most busy about another world."[1]
Matthew Henry

contents

#biblesays

"So here's what I want you to do, God helping you: Take your everyday, ordinary life – your sleeping, eating, going-to-work, and walking-around life – and place it before God as an offering."

romans chapter twelve verse one
the message

foreword

By Darlene Zschech

> "Spread love everywhere you go: First of all in your own house... let no one ever come to you without leaving better and happier. Be the living expression of God's kindness; kindness in your face, kindness in your eyes, kindness in your smile, kindness."
>
> Mother Theresa

There are many women who inspire me, and for many different reasons. One of the greats is Mother Theresa of course, whose life of complete devotion led to a revival of kindness and service to the poor; such a stunning reflection of Jesus Christ and His heart for humanity. And then there are the many women who cheer me on today, some from up close, and some from afar. Women who show a strength and resilience that defies their natural circumstances, and who consistently rise above the dull roar of opposition. And this is where my friend Di Wilson comes in.

Yes, she has done it again. This beautiful woman has written yet another no nonsense, practical and biblical blueprint for living life and ALL its myriad of challenges with joy, stability and great faith.

The reason I am writing this forward for Di, is that she writes with TRUTH. Her life and her message are one and the same. And for as long as I have known her, she has been one of the greatest champions of OTHERS that I've ever had the privilege of knowing. From her early days where she was trying to find her sense of purpose and confidence in the middle of what I witnessed as a VERY challenging time, to having to walk out the things in her heart with a strong and simple faith, even when she could not see what lay ahead.

To me she has always represented someone who has really YIELDED to Christ and all that that means.

I believe our hearts connected through testimony. Di hearing my story, me hearing hers. Two young women, sensing the call of God on our lives, on two opposite sides of the city of Sydney Australia, just walking it out. Kids on our hips, dreams in our hearts, God on our side.

Our stories, although different in detail, are also quite similar in the fact that if God can do it for us, work through us and by His grace even use us, then He can do it for you. This is the beauty and the power of GRACE. It weaves the miraculous into the fine details of the fallen, rendering the impossible possible, and even making swimming against the popular tide quite pleasurable. This is the power of testimony. LOVE IT!!!

As you read through these pages, I feel that you'll find a fresh sense of permission to wholly "go for the things in your heart that make you shine". It's your time...

We live in a world that is beyond desperate for truth, beyond desperate for answers, beyond desperate for true relationships and beyond desperate to live with a sense of purpose and value. And yet God Himself has placed us here, on purpose and for purpose, in this season of history, with His details in mind: to bring the light of Christ into all areas of life, from the mundane to the astounding.

So be prepared to be infused with life as you are encouraged through Di's story. For this is the story of God's leading and guiding, the story of truly falling trust first into God's mighty hand, and as you glean and learn from these powerful life lessons, I am confident that you will find new joy in truly becoming GONE...

With SO much love,

Darlene Zschech

the beginning

#anonymous

Jesus' hidden years ... and yours

"The Father's work in us does not sleep – though in spiritual winters he retracts all advertisement. And when He does so, He is purifying our faith, strengthening our character, conserving our energy, and preparing us for the future. The sleepy days of winter hide us so that the seductive days of summer will not ruin us."[2]

Alicia Britt Chole
Anonymous

introduction

#biblesays

"This is why the Father loves me: because I freely lay down my life. And so I am free to take it up again. No one takes it from me. I lay it down of my own free will. I have the right to lay it down; I also have the right to take it up again. I received this authority personally from my Father."

john chapter ten verses seventeen and eighteen
amplified version

Why. Should. I.

This is more a cry than a question; a statement spoken by humanity since the beginning of time; a protest of the will. We don't like to be told what to do, and in the event that we must be told what to do, we certainly always want to know why. Instinctively we are taught to fight and resist and never ever surrender our will. I often wonder where this inherent resistance to surrender comes from. We tend to resist flowing with anything we don't feel like doing, even if it could be the best idea of our life! Even as we approach the idea of GONE – the moment of surrender – this is no exception to our human condition of resistance.

Jesus surrendered all for us. Was he weak and mindless and unloved? No! He was and still is all-powerful, all knowing and altogether loved. Jesus' relationship with His Heavenly Father is key. Their love and trust are perfect. God's love is complete. Jesus' trust is complete. Imagine experiencing that level of love, and living in that level of trust. It is possible, but we won't experience it until, like Jesus, we have given the Father our all. Our moment of surrender will enable us to experience love like never before, and to trust like never before.

It's. My. Life.

Another cry of the human will. Yes, my life is my life, but this earth-life will not last forever. We have a choice to know Jesus now or know Him then, but we will all someday meet Him face to face and have to give an account for our life on earth. Will Jesus be a stranger or your Friend? The greatest privilege we have is to know Him now and make Him known to others.

Jesus is my hero – he has been my hero since I was a small child. I can't recall a time in my life when I didn't know Him as my best Friend. My Grandfather insisted that my parents take my sister and me to Sunday school every week because we needed God in our lives. My parents and my grandparents didn't go to church themselves so it was a miracle that together they decided it would be good for us kids to go. My Dad would drive up to the old stony church building and slow the car down long enough for my sister and me to jump out without getting hurt, but as soon as we were out and safely on the sidewalk, he would take off out of there as fast as he could so that a bolt of lightening wouldn't strike him down.

My beloved grandfather, Poppy, passed away when I was just 7 years old. It was the worst day of my seven-year life. He was my hero. I am sure that the reason I found it so easy to trust God, was because of my incredible grandfather and father.

The day my grandfather passed away was the day I found out about Heaven. I wasn't sure that I liked that place because I just wanted him to come home. Then I started to think and believe that somehow it might have been my fault that he had gone away to that place called Heaven. Maybe I wasn't a very good girl and maybe I caused something terrible to happen. I also discovered what guilt was that day. I was very overwhelmed with loss and grief and wished that I could take it all away.

Way before I could possibly comprehend the Holy Spirit's relationship with me, I can absolutely, without any shadow of doubt, completely and utterly recall His presence in my darkness. I have never been afraid of God or Jesus or the Holy Spirit. My whole experience in my relationship with the Trinity has been simple and clear. God loves me no matter what. Jesus is my best Friend. The Holy Spirit is always with me.

Our family somehow continued day after day to get on with our ordinary lives even though we would never be the same again without my grandfather with us. My grandmother never married again. They had 43 amazing years together and she then spent the remainder of her last twenty-nine years without him.

We spent a lot of time together as a family: my Mum and Dad, my sister and my grandmother, Nanny. One of the things we loved to do was go to the horse races. Nanny was part owner of two thoroughbred horses. We would often go on a Wednesday afternoon and most weekends. There were a few different racecourses we would frequent and one of them was Randwick. It was always so much fun to dress up and spend a day at the "races" with Nanny.

It was a Friday afternoon and my sister and I were getting ready for a special event. My sister's youth leader picked us up and drove us to church. My sister was now in Youth Group, but I was only twelve years old and wasn't "eligible" yet. It was 1979 and I found myself gathered onto a bus along with lots of teenagers and taken across the city of Sydney to a place I was very familiar with – Randwick Racecourse.

We walked from the bus to the grandstands. I had stood here before but this time my experience was very different. I had never seen the grandstands so full and there were people seated on the lawn area also. A man began to speak from a stage in the middle of the distant green. I can't recall what he said but I will never forget how I felt. At the end of his "speech" he talked about Jesus. He talked about Heaven and hell and he said that we needed to decide if we want to go to Heaven or hell. I knew right away I wanted to go to Heaven, because I wanted to be with Poppy again. I was still too young to really comprehend what was happening, but I was more than ready to experience my first encounter with Jesus my Savior. He had been my best Friend for years, but this was the first time I found out He could also be my Savior, my rescuer, my redeemer. The man then asked anyone who wanted to know Jesus as their Savior to come down the front, onto the lawn. He said over and over again, "Come to Jesus". I wanted to come to Jesus; He was my best Friend who was now going to save my life. The man who was speaking that night, inviting us to come to Jesus, was Rev Billy Graham. My life has never been the same since.

Jesus was now my best Friend and Savior but He was yet to become Lord. If we were to be truly honest about our relationship with our Maker, the challenge isn't with being friends, or with being "saved" and going to Heaven, our challenge is with the "Lord" aspect of our relationship. We love to be comforted, we love to be safe, but we don't much love to surrender.

My moment of surrender happened when I was sixteen years old. I was attending church one Sunday night and a visiting missionary was sharing his slides from a recent trip to Papua New Guinea. He wasn't very captivating in his presentation, in fact, how he looked was ordinary, how he spoke was ordinary, and his old-school slide show was very ordinary, but what he did was extra-ordinary. At the end of his presentation he asked for a response. He asked who would be prepared to go. I didn't quite know where "go" would ultimately lead me, but I knew it was my moment to go. As I stood to my feet and walked to the front of the altar, along with a few others beside me, the missionary man bent down onto his knees and one by one, prayed for each one of us to "go". He prayed that wherever our feet would go that we would bring the good news with us. Jesus was my best Friend. Jesus was my Savior. Now Jesus was my Lord and my life was complete.

I always believed from that moment that I would be a missionary somewhere in the world. I figured it could be Papua New Guinea or maybe India or Africa. I since learned that my most significant mission field would be my neighborhood at home. Being on mission isn't geographical, but rather it is all about being intentional. We can love our neighbor on the other side of the world and we can love our neighbor on the other side of the fence. When God sent us to Newport Beach, California to start a brand new church [Newport Church] we brought the spirit of being on mission with us; to love God with all our heart and soul, and to love our neighbors. It's easy to love strangers on the other side of the world, but to love our neighbors is the Gospel. My ordinary beginnings have helped me to stay longing for a simple life of faith and trust in God. Fast forward many decades now and I can say with humble sincerity that I love being GONE.

My husband Jonathan and I have six kids: his, hers and ours. We are a little like the Brady Brunch but without Alice. Our family was away in Memphis for a weekend, celebrating our twin sons Ben and Beau's 18th birthdays. We were out at a Brazilian steakhouse restaurant one evening – it was one of those places where the servers enthusiastically fill your plate with more food than anyone could possibly handle. It was a fun night, and as the evening went on, our youngest child London, who was four at the time, became tired and sleepy after a long day and eventful night. London comes with us wherever we go, and when it's time for her to go to sleep, she falls asleep wherever we are. So that night at the steakhouse, London crawled across her seat to my seat, and in no time at all she was asleep in my arms.

As she was falling asleep, I became acutely aware of the way her weight shifted as she transitioned from a state of wakefulness to complete slumber. When she was finally asleep, the deadweight, the weight of her body against mine, caused my legs to go numb. I had to move my arm and was quite uncomfortable because she was absolutely, totally and utterly, in that moment, GONE. She was fast asleep. As I looked into her beautiful little face, all I could think was that this is what the Lord means when he says, "Lay your life down." It should look like that peaceful picture of a child asleep in the arms of their loving parent. London was in a place where she could literally be completely abandoned, where she could be completely trusting. In that place, as I was holding her, she was completely peaceful, and her entire bodyweight had completely transferred over to me. She was completely GONE. She wasn't struggling, she wasn't having to get up to go to the dessert bar one more time. She was out like a light.

#gone

"The first eleven chapters of the book of Romans have provided the human being with everything they could ever want and it has all been based upon the work and person of the Lord Jesus. It is our natural instinct then to say that the process is complete. However, the apostle is beseeching us that the completeness of what we have been given should elicit a response. In the dispensation of Law the Jews worked for reward. In the dispensation of grace we should be working from gratitude."[1]

David Bayliss
Bible Scholar

As I held my daughter in my arms that night, I could not shake the thought that this is the stance our Heavenly Father wants us to have. Father God desires us to be completely abandoned, completely trusting, and completely at peace. He wants us to trust Him enough that we would be willing to transfer the full weight of our natural life onto His supernatural being. Our whole frame is under strain when we try to carry around our lives.

Inside the pages of GONE you will find words from one of my favorite books, "Anonymous," written by my friend Alicia Britt Chole. Reading Alicia's book changed my life. I had known the privilege of living a hidden, anonymous life, but hadn't quite understood the power of it. Alicia's words bring great perspective to our surrendered GONE life.

Being GONE is not about living the rest of our lives in a state of slumber! We don't need to have an eternal nap. What needs to lie down is our resistance. GONE is a revelation. When we voluntarily lay down our lives for Jesus, we are beneficiaries of His Kingdom. When we are completely surrendered, completely abandoned, when we are completely trusting, when we are completely at peace, the natural weight of our lives is transferred to a supernatural God. We are GONE.

It is the compassion that God has towards us that motivates us towards living "Romans 12 lives." Because of what God has done for us, our rightful response should be, "What can I do for Him?" If we don't understand that the complete work of Christ was accomplished to elicit our response, we will always be waiting for God to make another thing "happen" for us.

So often we want God to give us a warm fuzzy feeling, when what we really need to understand is that it has all already been done. It's finished. All we have to do now is decide to allow our Savior to become our Lord. We don't need God to do more in order for us to do more. The truth is, He has already done everything! All we need is simply to respond to Him! It's interesting that in this particular verse it is not our spirit that God is interested in, or our mind. It is our body. He says to lay it down. When it comes to us laying our lives down, it is not the thought that counts, it is the activity that counts. It is the giving of our everyday, ordinary lives; our sleeping, eating, going-to-work, and walking-around lives. We just need to place all of it, every day, before God as an offering.

When it comes to choosing our life's partner, the subject of surrender is all-important. GONE guy needs to find GONE girl so they can build an amazing GONE life together.

At some point, we are going to get to the end of our days [and let's pray that that day is a good long time away]. In the meantime, we've each been given an amazing and purposeful life on planet earth. All the good that we "thought" about doing is not what we are going to be rewarded for. It's going to require our whole being in living sacrifice for the Lord. This means responding, which means doing, which means being active. We need to understand that it isn't the thought that counts, it's the action that counts. Because of what God has done for us, our response should be: what can we do for Him?

What does a non-surrendered life look like?
- Pride
- Control
- Fear
- Guilt
- Ignorance

What does a surrendered life look like?
- Humility
- Trust
- Faith
- Peace
- Understanding

I've often wondered why surrender isn't a very popular idea. I think it is because people have thought that living the Christian life is all about sacrifice, but it's not. The Christian life is about surrender. The sacrifice has already been made! Jesus made the sacrifice, and our job is to respond out of gratitude. Jesus paid the price in one big sacrifice of surrender, once and for all, and all we need to do now is to lay ourselves down in His arms and transfer the weight of our lives to Him.

Inside the chapters of GONE you will find three clear pictures of life, along with choices we have to maximize our days on earth:

1. **MY OLD LIFE**
   This is our striving and strife-life, which will ultimately lead to burnout.

2. **MY NEW LIFE**
   This is our surrendered GONE life, which will ultimately lead to freedom and peace from the inside out.

3. **MY NOW LIFE**
   This is our meantime, which bridges our decision to surrender with the reality of our current life.

When we decide to be GONE with our old life, surrendered to our new life, while lovingly embracing our now life, that's when our dream life is set into motion. Life is a journey and the beginning of change sparks with a decision that we want to change. The grace of God abounds in our decision to surrender our lives, fully and completely to Jesus. God's great pleasure is to help us surrender.

When our little girl London laid down in my arms that night in Memphis, she wasn't under any kind of duress in doing so. She simply climbed onto my lap and fell asleep. Completely abandoned, completely trusting, completely at peace. With simple faith and trust, she surrendered her tired little body. She was weightless and fearless. She was GONE.

London's surrender was progressive, as was mine. She approached a familiar lap – mine. I approached a familiar friend – Jesus. She was going. I was going. London lay her head down, about to fall asleep. I bowed my head in prayer to receive Jesus as my Savior. She was going, going. I was going, going. London finally surrendered in sleep. I finally surrendered my life when Jesus became my Lord. She was going, going, GONE. My progressive surrender experience was one of going, going, GONE.

My prayer is that you too will be inspired to have faith and trust implicitly in your relationship with your Maker. May you love deeply and eternally your moment of surrender; your moment of GONE.

#biblesays

"The faithful love of the Lord never ends! His mercies never cease. Great is his faithfulness; His mercies begin afresh each morning."

lamentations chapter three verses twenty-two to twenty-three new living translation

my
old life

#anonymous

Jesus' hidden years ... and yours

"Have you ever felt hidden? Have you ever moved to a new place or entered a new environment where no one knew who you were, what you could do, or what dreams ignited your soul? Have you ever crossed the threshold into another season of life, like parenthood or extended studies, where you shifted from recognition to anonymity, from the court to the bench, from standing as a leader to sitting as a learner again? Have you ever resigned or retired from a position or title and transitioned from being sought out to left out, consulted to unconsidered, celebrated to celebrating others? In these hidden seasons, we are more familiar with being invisible than acclaimed. Concealed for months or years or decades, our potential seems to hibernate like a bear in winter, and over time we begin to wonder if spring will ever awaken it again. Hidden hopes. Hidden dreams. Hidden gifts..."[2]

Alicia Britt Chole
Anonymous

exhaustion of emotional and or physical strength usually as a result
of prolonged stress or frustration

#biblesays

"What I don't understand about myself is that I decide one way, but then I act another, doing things I absolutely despise... So if I can't be trusted to figure out what is best for myself and then do it, it becomes obvious that God's command is necessary. But I need something more! ... I obviously need help! I realize that I don't have what it takes. I can will it, but I can't do it. I decide to do good, but I don't really do it; I decide not to do bad, but then I do it anyway. My decisions, such as they are, don't result in actions. Something has gone wrong deep within me and gets the better of me every time. It happens so regularly that it's predictable... Parts of me covertly rebel, and just when I least expect it, they take charge. I've tried everything and nothing helps. I'm at the end of my rope. Is there no one who can do anything for me? Isn't that the real question?"

romans chapter seven verses fifteen to twenty-five
the message

Burnout.

The enemy wants to take you out from the inside. He would love for you to have woken up this morning and to have pressed the snooze button on the rest of your life.

We have all had times where we've come to the end of our rope. My hope is that those times would be minimized in our life. If you feel like you're at the end of your rope and you're about to jump – here is some good news from that passage of scripture that is the answer to our dilemma, "That Jesus Christ can and does. He acted to set things right in this life of contradictions..."

If we go to anyone but Jesus when we're at the end of our rope, we will most likely jump! He is the only one Who can only make sense of this life full of contradictions, an internal war we all face.

What is burnout?

- The reduction of a fuel or substance to nothing through use or combustion.
- Exhaustion of emotional and or physical strength usually as a result of prolonged stress or frustration.
- Burnout is a psychological term for the experience of long-term exhaustion and diminished interest.
- Burnout is not a recognized disorder although it is recognized as, "Problems related to life-management difficulty."

Let me ask you a question. If your car runs out of gas while you are driving it, whose fault is that? When we get into a car and think we can drive down the freeway on empty, and then run out of gas, there is no point in calling our mother, brother, or pastor, and blaming them. There is no point in calling our boss, our friend, or our child. Who was driving the car? The driver was driving the car. When we find ourselves in the driver's seat of life and we don't take care that we have ample fuel for the journey ahead, we will simply burnout. And that will be no one's fault but our own.

#biblesays

"Are you tired? Worn out? Burned out on religion? Come to me. Get away with me and you'll recover your life. I'll show you how to take a real rest. Walk with me and work with me—watch how I do it. Learn the unforced rhythms of grace. I won't lay anything heavy or ill-fitting on you. Keep company with me and you'll learn to live freely and lightly."

matthew chapter eleven verses twenty-eight to thirty
the message

Inside an aircraft, there are oxygen masks that drop down from overhead in case of emergency – you're meant to apply the mask to yourself before you can assist someone else with theirs. You need to look after yourself, and take personal responsibility for your life. When you lack time and energy in personal reserve, that's a problem. It is my responsibility to look after myself.

Burnout always involves feelings:

- Feelings of always giving and not receiving.
- Feelings that what you signed up for isn't now what you really want.
- Feelings your contribution doesn't really count.
- Feelings of resentment towards the people you serve.
- Feelings of others being "overly" concerned for you.
- Feelings of self-protection and self-deflection.
- Feelings of the need to pursue one's personal happiness more than one's purpose.
- Feelings of the need to blame burnout on everyone else.
- Feelings of being overwhelmed beyond our capacity.
- Feelings of being emotionally/spiritually empty.
- Feelings of wanting to run away.

Burnout always involves feelings. If the devil knows that you live by your feelings, he will feed you everything you feel like.

Let's take a look at "Burnout Syndrome."[1] Psychologists have theorized that the burnout process can be categorized into many phases, as follows:

1. The compulsion to prove oneself.
   If we are excessively ambitious, we will burnout.

2. Working harder.
   If we are obsessive about doing everything yourself, we will burn out.

3. Neglecting personal needs.
   When we lack time and energy in personal reserve, that's a problem. It is my responsibility to look after myself.

4. Displacement of conflicts.
   This means that we are now unable to see and acknowledge the source of the problem.

5. Revision of values.
   This occurs when someone shifts or completely changes their value system, sometimes beyond recognition

6. Denial of emerging problems.
   When you are in denial, you are absolutely intolerant of any intervention, citing any offer of assistance as "interference."

7. Withdrawal.
   Withdrawal is a telltale sign and it leads to isolation and hopelessness in a person's life.

8. Obvious behavioral changes.
   By this stage in the burnout process, family and friends are no longer able to cover for behavioral changes.

9. Depersonalization.
   Total focus on achieving present goals, and complete disconnection with future consequences.

10. Inner emptiness.
    Filling the void with any number of things such as unhealthy relationships, overeating, sex, alcohol, drugs.

#gone

"Never was so much owed by so many to so few."[2]

Winston Churchill

We know why ordinary, everyday people suffer from burnout, but why do "Christians" suffer from burnout?

- Unhelpful priorities.
- Unhelpful motivation.
- Unhelpful relationships.
- Unhelpful attitude.
- Unresolved internal compromise.
- Unresolved internal contradictions.
- Unresolved internal conflict.

We have to deal with our heart and our soul. We can't let our emotions be like a runaway train about to crash.

The enemy is after our integrity – he'd love for you to live a life of compromise, because a life of compromise robs you of your peace. The enemy is also after our certainty, and would love for you to feel confused, feeling like you can't make a decision about anything. Confusion will cause you to burn out. That's not God! God gives us very clear instruction. Don't be confused - be confident! The enemy is after our serenity.

If the enemy can get us to give up and shut up on the inside, and walk away on the outside, he has won! God needs an army who won't give up and won't walk away. We have much to do, we have many people to reach and help and we have to be counted among the few who stay strong! In 40 years of knowing Jesus, in 40 years of going to church and in 20 years of ministry, I have experienced many of the "feelings" that have come to us all, I can honestly say I have never been "burnt out." There has to be a reason. I have talked to some of my ministry friends about it. We just don't allow burnout.

3 KEYS TO STAYING STRONG

1. Serve God.
   By serving God you are going to stay strong.

#biblesays

"Those of us who are strong and able in the faith need to step in and lend a hand to those who falter, and not just do what is most convenient for us. Strength is for service, not status. Each one of us needs to look after the good of the people around us, asking ourselves, "How can I help?" That's exactly what Jesus did. He didn't make it easy for himself by avoiding people's troubles, but waded right in and helped out. "I took on the troubles of the troubled," is the way Scripture puts it. Even if it was written in Scripture long ago, you can be sure it's written for us. God wants the combination of his steady, constant calling and warm, personal counsel in Scripture to come to characterize us, keeping us alert for whatever he will do next. May our dependably steady and warmly personal God develop maturity in you so that you get along with each other as well as Jesus gets along with us all. Then we'll be a choir—not our voices only, but our very lives singing in harmony in a stunning anthem to the God and Father of our Master Jesus!"

romans chapter fifteen verses one to five
the message

Jesus is the best example of someone who had the potential to burn out, but didn't. Don't you think He might have felt a little bit overwhelmed by the crowds, pressured by people, pressured by the time He knew He didn't have to do all the things He thought He might do? If Jesus is our example and He did not burn out, then we can look forward to a life refreshed in Him rather than one that is drained. You just have to see it differently. Don't look at it as being draining, look at it as being refreshing. So what do we need to do?

We need to serve more, not less.

We need to serve God, not man.

Let's look at an example. If your cell phone was to ring, and you saw that God was calling, you would pick up! If your cell phone rings and you see it's your leader calling most likely asking you to serve, you might hit decline! When someone asks you to serve, and you do it as unto the Lord, you won't burnout. It's only when we start serving "man" that we will burnout.

We need to serve God, not ourselves.

2. Unload on God.

Have you ever felt like throwing a pot or a pan at someone's head? The Bible says to pile all our troubles on God, to throw our worries and cares on Him, rather than throwing it all on our kids, our husband, or our friends. Sometimes we need to "bite it 'til it bleeds" [our tongue]. We can throw it at Him and pile it on Him. If we don't, we will enter the danger zone in our relationships. God can handle your issues.

- Your Mamma can't handle them.
- Your girlfriend or boyfriend can't handle them.
- Your husband or wife can't handle them.
- You can't handle them.

Our God can handle anything we throw His way.

#biblesays

"Throw all your worry on Him, because He cares for you."

one peter chapter five verse seven
international standard version

"Pile your troubles on God's shoulders – He'll carry your load He'll help you out. He'll never let good people topple into ruin."

psalm chapter fifty-five verse twenty-two
the message

3. Get away with God.

My husband loves to get away. He loves "Travel and Leisure Magazine", and we spend time talking about trips that we're going to take and destinations to visit. But the reason he loves to get away with me is to relax. He knows during our time away I'm not going to mow him down with my emotions. If he thought that he had to take me away to fix me, then he would do anything possible not to go anywhere with me. If you're going to have a relaxing vacation, do it from a place of strength.

Get away with Jesus and get yourself sorted out. We go to the beautician and we get our hair done, we do our nails, and then go on our vacation but we are a nightmare to be around because we haven't been away with Jesus. We need to get away with Jesus, and then we'll bless our family and our friends. It's great to have beautiful hair and beautiful nails, but if you have given your Bible time to your beautician, then you have your priorities mixed up.

If you don't read the Bible and you only listen to your friends, it's only a matter of time before you might be taken out - taken out of your destiny, taken out of what God wants for your life and taken out of any happiness that you could possibly have.

Be very aware of people who cut in on you. Years ago, phones were connected to party lines. One could be talking on the phone and all of a sudden you might hear someone else on the line talking as well. They cut in on you and suddenly the lines were crossed. Do not accept it when somebody cuts across what God is doing in your life in order to take you in a different direction. You need to see this as serious interference. The enemy wants to take you out. Don't let people cut in on you. You have permission to push back.

A life of surrender is a life of true freedom. When we choose to be GONE in Him, we choose a life of internal energy that comes from our relationship with Jesus, and that amazing energy never burns out.

#biblesays

"You were running superbly! Who cut in on you, deflecting you from the true course of obedience? This detour doesn't come from the One who called you into the race in the first place. And please don't toss this off as insignificant. It only takes a minute amount of yeast, you know, to permeate an entire loaf of bread. Deep down, the Master has given me confidence that you will not defect. But the one who is upsetting you, whoever he is, will bear the divine judgment."

galatians chapter five verses seven to ten
the message

my
new life

#gone

"Imagine there is a bank which credits your account each morning with $86,400, carries over no balance from day to day, allowing you to keep no cash balance, and every evening cancels whatever part of the amount you had failed to use during the day. What would you do? Draw out every cent, of course! Well, everyone has such a bank. Its name is TIME. Every morning, it credits you with 86,400 seconds. Every night it writes off, as lost, whatever of this you have failed to invest to good purpose. It carries over no balance. It allows no overdraft. Each day it opens a new account for you. Each night it burns the records of the day. If you fail to use the day's deposits, the loss is yours. There is no going back. There is no drawing against the tomorrow. You must live in the present on today's deposits. Invest it so as to get from it the utmost in health, happiness and success! The clock is running. Make the most of today."[1]

email from a friend
with love

everyday

happening each day; commonplace or usual; routine; habitual

The alarm goes off. Same time. Everyday.

The more mornings I awake, the more I realize that the alarm going off at the same time everyday, is actually a friend rather than an enemy. Would I occasionally like to go to sleep and have no alarm to set for the morning? Absolutely. Occasionally, yes; everyday, no.

Everyday is a gift from God, full of potential. Everyday is worth getting out of bed for. Everyday, we should be filled with expectation, building our lives according to the patterns set out for us in God's Word – the Bible. Everyday, we should embrace routine, habitual customs that cause our lives to increase and flourish. So many times we miss opportunities to build our lives because we miss the value of everyday.

We need to realize the value of:

- ONE minute
- ONE hour
- ONE day
- ONE month
- ONE year
- ONE life

As a wife and Mum, I've come to really value routine in my everyday life. Routine helps me make room for spontaneity. Routine helps me guide my family with stability. To me, routine isn't boring. It is essential to success and significance. The routine of our everyday life is the backbone to our existence. We don't build our lives going from special event to special event. We build our lives by consistently choosing positive habits everyday.

I will never forget the elation of giving birth the first time. It was twins! Although I bask in the memory of this particularly special moment in my life, I most certainly would not want to give birth to twins everyday. We have highlights in our lifetime that are "mid-points." The day we start school, our first boyfriend, passing our drivers license test, graduation, our first job, getting married, our first promotion, having our first baby, birthdays, anniversaries, and all kinds of celebrations. We also have our everyday, ordinary life. And that makes up the majority of our days. We choose what we will do with those days; those days aren't particularly pretty or special or celebrated.

We are a product of our decisions. In each moment that passes, we have the ability to create our lives. Each decision creates habits, and these habits in our everyday lives form patterns of behavior. We can either intentionally create positive habits that help us move towards our dreams, or we can go through life without direction while we incidentally develop habits returning less than favorable results.

Our daily success is determined by our daily activities. Making the decision to create great habits will build your life. We need motivation to get us started, but it is positive habits that keep us going everyday. It is important to create a clear vision for all aspects of your life: body, soul and spirit. Write down what you want for your relationships, your finances, your career, your mission, your ministry.

What we do regularly is more important than what we do occasionally. What we do routinely is more important than what we do sometimes. By applying steady and consistent focus to something everyday, we have a better chance at accomplishment.

So how do we begin to contemplate a life of service in deep gratitude for all that God has done for us? We begin by waking up everyday and recognizing it as a gift from God, for God. Everyday. In our everyday lives; in our commonplace activities; in our routine daily customs; in our everyday habitual places and practices.

Today is a gift from God, for God. Not everybody wakes up and recognizes that today is a gift from God, let alone for God. In case you're wondering what you're meant to be doing with your life, or what this day is for, it is for God. To sulk through a moment or to have a bad day is to waste a moment, to waste a day. Every single day is a gift.

#

Develop a list of everyday routine activities to help you reach your visionary goals.

1. Frame your day with positive thoughts and vision for the future.

2. Set your alarm to maximize your morning and your day.

3. Read your Bible everyday and pray everyday.

4. Exercise regularly. Sow energy and you will reap energy.

5. Clean as you go through your house so that Home Beautiful is your goal rather than housework being a big event.

6. De-clutter your home and work space and have a place for everything.

7. Write lists and check lists so you aren't relying on memory.

8. Prepare food before you need it so you aren't starving by mealtime and eat the wrong types of food.

9. Be 10 minutes early rather than 5 minutes late [with a coffee in your hand].

10. Take time to connect with family and friends. Sprinkle the love regularly so family won't feel as though they are another special event in your life.

If every single day is a gift and we squander it, then shame on us. And if it's His gift and we have a bad day, shame on us, because we don't need to have a bad day. Have a "not great" moment if you must, but please don't have an hour, or a night, or an entirely "bad" day!

A bad day can be triggered by unresolved issues from the night before. A bad day can be triggered and lengthened by unresolved issues with people in our everyday world. We need to make a decision to simply stop and start again.

Every day is a gift from God, for God. Therefore I cannot afford to be rehearsing pain every day. Therefore I cannot keep longing to go back in time every day. We don't need to go back to our past, but instead use the gift that is today to press on toward the future. I also cannot keep longing to go to a future time that I am not yet prepared for. I have today, and that is all I have! We need to ask ourselves how much of our every day is spent on living surrendered to God for God. If we do not recognize our life as a gift from God, it's going to be very hard to give it to God. Every single one of our days should be lived for God. We very simply begin by taking our everyday life and placing it before God as an offering. When we give our everyday to the Lord, it helps us remember that we are not alone, that Jesus is with us every step of the way through our day. Living with that kind of revelation and understanding helps us to make wise choices and stay out of trouble. Trouble? Yes, trouble! A troubled soul lives a troubled life. A positive soul lives a positive life. We need to do whatever we can in our everyday life to bring positivity in and to get the trouble out.

In this season of my life, at the time of writing this book, our twin boys Ben and Beau are transitioning from school life to college life. They are transitioning, and I am transitioning. I don't complain about getting up at 5.20am to make breakfast for my kids because I'm happy about it, and you can't complain about what you're happy about! So if you're not happy about something, get happy!

What does your everyday look like? Everyone's life is different.

Here's a glimpse into mine:

- 5.20 am alarm
- Tea [one cup to wake up, second cup to get me up]
- Bible in a Year daily devotional reading
- Breakfast Club for my kids
- Home Beautiful
- School run
- Cardio
- Getting Ready
- Work
- School run
- Kids
- Dinner
- Family time and relax time
- Work
- Sleep

The reason I'm so happy about getting up at that hour is because I still have kids at home. While they are still at home, I'm making the most of my everyday, and I am going to be a mother who was, and is, consistent. What good is it if mom tells everyone else what they should be doing to help others, but in her own home she can't get out of bed to connect with her kids every day? I know what it's going to take for my kids to have a good memory of their Mom. I understand that. I do have to turn myself inside out sometimes, but at the end of the day, I also know I can't recreate my kids' memories. Today is the time for creating memories that will be stored up for my tomorrows, and theirs. I know that my everyday investment into my kids' lives is something that I will reap for eternity.

At 5.20am my alarm goes off each morning, and my husband Jonathan makes me a cup of tea – to wake me up. Ten minutes later, he will make me a second cup of tea – this time to get me up. I will then go downstairs to prepare for breakfast: lamps on, candles lit, coffee brewing, breakfast cooking, Pandora playing. There isn't much conversation at that time of the day but at least I know I'm there in case one strikes up. A kiss goodbye on the cheek from each kid on their way out the door begins the next part of the morning. Afterwards I proceed with "Home Beautiful" – a term I coined many years ago when I realized how un-motivating the word "cleaning" is. Cleaning is what you have to do. "Home Beautiful" is what you want to achieve. I love to focus on goals, so when I am "cleaning" I am producing "Home Beautiful."

Somewhere before taking our youngest child to school, I'll read my Bible, and then I'll do my cardio – either elliptical for 40 minutes or a good brisk outdoor run for 35 minutes. I then shower and get ready for my work day which usually starts at 8.30am. London's school finishes early so I need to pack as much work into my day as possible. When London is home it is London time. When Ben, Beau and Bella are home, it is Ben, Beau and Bella time. When Jonathan is home and needs me, it is husband time. Period. I love to cook and dinner is always a highlight in our day, especially when we can co-ordinate for all to be at home at the same time. I do find time to relax, and it's usually at the very end of the night when I switch on a cooking show and zone out watching all the food that I wish I could eat! Then, I go to sleep. Finally.

That's my day. It's routine. There is much healthy routine in my life that I'm grateful for. And when there is routine in your life, there's an awareness of how that routine frames your life.

As well as being a wife, a mother and an author, I am also a pastor - but there was once a time when I wasn't a pastor. I was a kid. I wasn't a pastor's kid; I was just a kid. I did my own thing and I woke up whenever I wanted to. Back in those days, 12noon was my 5.20am! There then came a time when I felt the call to respond to everything God had done for me. I was still a teenager, but all of a sudden I was a teenager with a reason to get out of bed. We don't simply wake up one day and become someone highly committed to purpose. I learned to dedicate my days to God for His purpose long before I became a pastor.

We don't need a badge or title to surrender our lives to Jesus. We just need to respond to all He has surrendered for us. As long as everything we do in our everyday life is in broad-strokes all about our purpose in Him, we are going to live significant, surrendered lives. This everyday surrendered life isn't reserved for the "elite troops" or people who are paid to lay their lives down. This life is for all who understand and embrace voluntary surrender.

Ever since I have had a revelation of giving my life away everyday, I have only benefited from it. I cannot encourage you enough to make the transition to living your everyday life, which is from God, for God – everyday! Giving your life away isn't about sacrifice, it's about response and benefits. When we kiss our old life goodbye, we lose the weight of trying to make it on our own. When we kiss our old life goodbye, we rest in our Maker's arms, the deadweight GONE and our spirit, soul and body – alive and kicking – and moving forward.

What does your everyday look like? Everyday the sun rises. Everyday the sun sets. Everyday we wake up. Everyday we go to sleep. Everyday we speak up. Everyday we keep quiet. Everyday we inhale. Everyday we exhale. Everyday comes with the opportunity to give and to receive. God created our everyday before time began. He knows every detail of our everyday. He cares about our everyday. He loves for us to be in His arms everyday.

If we consider the highlight days in our lives, we can create more of them by developing a strong awareness of everyday being a gift from God, for God. There are certain days when we are very aware that this particular day is a gift from God, and we are giving it back to God - when we take part in an outreach day, for example, or when we are in His house on a Sunday morning.

#biblesays

"So don't you see that we don't owe this old do-it-yourself life one red cent. There's nothing in it for us, nothing at all. The best thing to do is give it a decent burial and get on with your new life. God's Spirit beckons. There are things to do and places to go!"

romans chapter eight verses twelve to fourteen
the message

The Bible doesn't say to offer only our special occasion days in a spiritual context. Everyday highlights for me include making sure I tell my loved ones I love them. Everyday highlights for me include being creative in problem solving so I don't experience going around the same mountains everyday. Everyday highlights for me are when I meet new friends at my kids' school, and when I remember their name the next time I see them. Everyday highlights for me are when my spirit and soul become illuminated when I read my Bible, everyday. It is our everyday life that God is interested in.

Even those days we find extremely challenging, that we wish we could change, have the potential to become extraordinary in God's hands. It is the everyday [I don't like today]. It is the everyday [I wish today would change]. It is the everyday [I wish I had more money]. It is the everyday [I wish I had a different job]. It is the everyday [I wish I had a different life]. Maybe that's how you've been feeling, that life seems hopeless. Let me assure you that your worst day GONE will be better than your best day not completely surrendered to God.

God created our everyday before time began. He knows every detail of our everyday. He cares about our everyday.

God wants us to be in his arms everyday. Everyday is a gift from God for God. We just need to respond appropriately to the gift and then we enjoy the benefits. The Father wants to give you the very Kingdom itself. When London was asleep in my arms at the restaurant that night in Memphis, I was presented with such a vivid visual for the fully surrendered, GONE life. As London lay there, she didn't feel the need to get up and struggle to try and make her own way home. She didn't get up and feel the need to go and solve the world's problems. She was just out. She was GONE.

If we can live in that permanent state where we are GONE and we stay GONE, and let God take care of business – everyday – our life will change for the better.

#biblesays

"What I'm trying to do here is get you to relax, not be so preoccupied with getting so you can respond to God's giving. People who don't know God and the way he works fuss over these things, but you know both God and how he works. Steep yourself in God-reality, God-initiative, God-provisions. You'll find all your everyday human concerns will be met. Don't be afraid of missing out. You're my dearest friends! The Father wants to give you the very Kingdom itself."

luke chapter twelve verses twenty-nine to thirty two
the message

Life only gets messy, weighty, and hard when we keep resurrecting our old life and attempt to use all our old responses. We can end up losing whole days and whole weeks!

When we worry, we carry around dead weight. The Bible clearly says that we shouldn't worry about anything but instead we should pray about everything. Prayer shifts the weight of our cares from off of our shoulders, and onto God's. Prayer fills us with peace so we are no longer burdened with worry. When we hold onto resentment, we carry around dead weight. The Bible says that we should forgive others because we have received forgiveness from God. Forgiveness shifts the weight from pain to peace. When we pursue doing our own thing, we carry around dead weight. The Bible says that we should trust in the Lord and then He will grant us the desires of our heart. Trusting God shifts the weight from striving to peace.

We need to trust God. Most of us already know that, but how can we rise above the loud voices of worry that crowd our thoughts and just jump over to a position of trust? It's actually not that complicated. Maybe right now just take a deep breath and relax, take a moment to stop the worrying thoughts and hear your Father saying, "Relax." If peace is our goal, we can be assured that we will be the beneficiaries of peace when we relax and surrender all. Our posture should be to receive what God has for us everyday. This is about being positioned to receive rather than being preoccupied with getting. Perhaps you find this concept challenging because past experiences may have taught you that if you don't make things happen, nothing good will come your way. Perhaps hard times have caused you to become preoccupied with "getting" in order to survive. We need to learn to respond out of our spirit; not out of our flesh, not out of our fear, not out of a hard season. It is this day and everyday that the Lord has made. Everyday we need to begin. Everyday we need to continue. Everyday we need to become. Everyday is a new day; a blank canvas. We choose who we want to be. We choose where we want to go.

#biblesays

"This is the day the LORD has made. We will rejoice and be glad in it."

psalm one hundred and eighteen verse twenty-four
new international version

We choose how we want to live – everyday. Let's fill ourselves with the Word of God so that we can have some context and strength in our lives. Everyday, it's a new day. We get to choose who we want to be, where we want to go, how we want to live, everyday. You might feel confined and unable to make choices that will get you where you want to go. You can choose your way out of where you are now. You might not see your life change overnight, but you can change slowly and steadily if you continue to stay GONE in his arms.

I have the privilege of visiting a group of women in Chino Women's Prison in Southern California every month. These women are behind bars because they have been convicted for murdering their abusive spouses. Some have been in there for over thirty years. What is most amazing to me is to observe some of their attitudes on how they spend their lives everyday. Some are depressed and do nothing everyday. Others have made decisions to make the most of their everyday to either help themselves or help others. Hundreds of women, all experiencing the same circumstances, living very different versions of "life on the inside." And it all has to do with perspective. It has everything to do with the value they believe God places upon their seconds, minutes, hours, weeks, months, and years regardless of where they are spent.

We have more choices to change our lives than we realize. To decide to live the surrendered – GONE – life is the best choice you could ever make! Everyday filled with purpose, everyday filled with solution, everyday filled with accomplishment, everyday filled with adventure, everyday filled with peace.

When London was just a toddler, she nearly lost her finger in a nasty accident at home when it was slammed in a quarter inch glass shower door. She was only two years old at the time and came running out with blood all over her face. I wasn't sure where the blood was coming from, and I almost passed out! We took London straight to the emergency room at the Children's Hospital. It was one of the most traumatic experiences I have ever faced. The doctors wanted to medicate me to calm me down!

Before they could get to work fixing London's finger, they needed to make sure she would stay still. They wrapped her up in a tiny straitjacket and asked me to gently lie on top of her so she would feel comforted and also be restrained from moving. I'll never forget how upset London was during those moments at the hospital. She kept saying "No, no, no! Mummy, let me go, let me go, let me go!" Thankfully, she was able to keep her finger, but if she had not been able to stay still, she may have lost it.

Because London was in deep pain, deep turmoil, and great need, she resisted just lying there allowing me to take care of things for her. She kept trying to get up and fix things for herself. Of course I knew she had no ability to do anything remotely useful for her pain. Any attempts she could have made would have brought her to even more pain – or worse! As a parent there was nothing I wouldn't do to still my daughter so the doctors could continue to do their work of fixing and healing her. In spite of her most furious efforts to escape the pain, I held her down only because I love her. I knew that making her endure that temporary pain would ultimately lead to her complete wholeness. She didn't understand it at all, but I did. It was my faithfulness that forced her to be still during the pain so that she could come out healthy and whole on the other side. I will never forget that day. It will forever remind me of the faithfulness of God. When we are helpless, He is faithful. I just need to remain GONE in Him.

We have God on our side. If you have pain: physical, emotional or both, if you have turmoil, and if you have great needs, stay down. Stay GONE. Let God heal you, let Him work on your behalf. By all means, be active in prayer. Be proactive. Let your spirit do the leading in everything you need to do, but don't wrestle with God. Stay GONE Allow God to work in you, and to work on your behalf.

"You are never too old to set another goal or to dream a new dream."[2]
C.S. Lewis

"The remarkable thing is, we have a choice everyday regarding the attitude we will embrace for that day."[3]
Charles Swindoll

"Everything you now do is something you have chosen to do. Some people don't want to believe that. But if you're over age twenty-one, your life is what you're making of it. To change your life, you need to change your priorities."[4]
John Maxwell

"If you don't know where you are going, how can you expect to get there?"[5]
Basil S. Walsh

"Goals are dreams with deadlines."[6]
Diana Scharf Hunt

"Good habits, once established, are just as hard to break as bad habits."[7]
Robert Puller

"We are what we repeatedly do. Excellence, then, is not an act, but a habit."[8]
Aristotle

#gone

Following are some questions to ask yourself EVERYDAY:

1.   What attitude will I embrace today?

2.   What are my priorities today?

3.   Where am I going today?

4.   What are my goals today?

5.   What good habits am I establishing today?

6.   What will I do repeatedly today?

7.   Who can I help today?

Perhaps you have not realized that every day is a gift from God, and God has given it to you so you can set another goal and dream a bigger dream. Imagine if today was the day of your greatest purpose, and you woke up and treated it like it was just another day? We need to understand and appreciate that every single day matters to God and it should also matter to us. Every day is a gift from God so we can set another goal and dream a bigger dream. If someone comes alongside you and tries to hijack a portion of your day, please don't give them the whole thing. Your day is a gift from God, for God. You might ask, where is God when someone is giving me a hard time? He's there, waiting for you to respond to Him. Instead of spending all of our time and energy responding to any nonsense that might be happening in our lives, we need to allocate time and energy to responding to God. The following are some important highlights we can create in our life, everyday:

1. Pray EVERYDAY
    Remember to talk to God. Prayer doesn't need to feel intense. It's also good to talk to people who regularly talk to God, because they are more likely to give you wise counsel when you need it!

2. Say I love you EVERYDAY
    Perhaps you were raised with parents who didn't say, "I love you." We need to say it. Say I love you.

3. Forgive quickly EVERYDAY
    Someone once said, "Life becomes easier when you learn to accept an apology you never got."

4. Work hard EVERYDAY
    The Bible says to do it! There are so many beautiful scriptures about work - especially in Proverbs. I think it's fantastic!

#biblesays

"Jesus said, 'If I turned the spotlight on myself, it wouldn't amount to anything.'"

john chapter eight verse fifty-four
the message

#gone

BE A LEADER

1.   Think the best of others.

2.   Think and speak positive words.

3.   Think through decisions.

4.   Think about what I do have.

5.   Think #biblesays.

6.   Think about God and His Sovereignty.

7.   Think good thoughts today.

Jonathan Wilson

5. Be productive EVERYDAY

I love working hard when it produces! There's nothing better than being in production mode and having it be fruitful! At the end of the day, we want to see a return for our effort.

6. Be physically active EVERYDAY

You don't have to exercise every day - I take a Sabbath break and here's why: the reason I don't exercise seven days a week is because if I did and then dropped down to six days a week later on, I know I'd feel really disappointed in myself. Think about it! If we max ourselves out to achieve some extreme goal, then we can potentially lose our peace over anything that we do afterwards that is not at the same level. We need to be wise. Do something everyday that you know is going to help you to stay focused on this gift of everyday. Another thing I don't do everyday is weigh myself. I know some people are surprised to know I only weigh myself twice a year. I'm not recommending everyone should do the same. If you're on a weight-loss program, you should be weighing yourself as often as you need to make sure you track your progress. Since I'm not on a weight-loss program now, I don't need to know that my fluids are up two to three pounds. That little fact could cause me to lose my focus for a day! I don't want to lose one single day. I can't live like that, and I'm sure my family doesn't want me to, so if my jeans fit, I'm good!

7. Make wise choices with food EVERYDAY

Notice I didn't say "eat healthy" everyday. It's virtually impossible to eat healthy everyday, but it is absolutely possible and essential for our well being, that we make wise choices with food everyday. So having a splurge is not a problem, but choosing to splurge because you have a plan to be extra careful the next day and week ahead is wisdom. I have had to work hard in this area and I understand the importance of making wise choices with food everyday. Eating mainly fresh food is wise, as is being sure to read the ingredients on anything packaged. Also be aware of when you eat and how much you are eating. Here's a basic plan:

Breakfast: eggs

Snack: protein drink and an apple

Lunch: lean protein and green vegetables

Snack: protein drink and an apple

Dinner: lean protein and green vegetables

             [drink lots of water too, everyday]

8. Be thankful EVERYDAY

You have nothing to complain about when you're thankful. Sometimes we're much more aware of what we don't have rather than all we do have. It's worth the effort to be thankful for all we have that others may not. If the job you have is not your dream job, please be thankful you have a job! If your husband doesn't do enough around the house, please be thankful that you have a husband. If your kids make a mess, please be thankful you have kids. I actually love picking up after my kids because I love my kids. I love having kids, and I'm happy to do it. People in our everyday lives find thankfulness so magnetic and energizing.

9. Do the right thing EVERYDAY

Do the right thing even if it means it will be to your own hurt. Obedience is less painful than regret. If you say you're going to do something, do it. If you say you're going to show up, show up. If you said you're going to pay for it, pay for it. If you said you were going to complete a project, complete it. Do the right thing! We need to learn that it's more important for us to do the right thing than to correct someone else's poor behavior. We should be more concerned with our choices to do the right thing rather than whether or not others have done the wrong or right thing. Doing what is right is not always easy. Also, doing what is right is sometimes not acknowledged nor appreciated. If we are prepared to do the right thing we also need to be prepared to do the right thing anonymously. No spotlights, no applause, no awards. When you live surrendered – GONE – you live with the benefit of knowing your rewards come from Heaven not earth.

10. Give your life away EVERYDAY

God, in His infinite wisdom, saw fit to give us our lives one day at a time, EVERYDAY. Sometimes we want to skip some days and go back to others. The truth is that we can't use a remote control and change the channel of our lives. God is in control and He says to make the most of today, everyday. His perfect measure is our everyday. Our lives have infinite value! In God's hands our lives are maximized to impact more than we now realize. We don't have a day to waste. Everyday is a gift from God, for God.

I saw a movie once where the main character was given a remote control in which he could fast forward his life. He chose to fast-forward elements of his life that he felt at the time were boring; his everyday, ordinary life. But then like most household appliances, his remote began to malfunction and he was stuck with the consequences. God has given us our everyday as a gift; He intentionally created us as finite beings that cannot jump around to whatever part of life we choose at any moment.

Our everyday life, every moment of every day is to be presented to God, no fast-forwarding, no pause button.

I am so grateful for being married to such an amazing Godly man who exemplifies Christ-like leadership not just in our church but in our home, everyday. He inspires and encourages me everyday to be a leader. When life becomes stressful, hurtful, unpredictable and sometimes plain awful, he reminds me to be a leader. He doesn't just remind me by dropping subtle hints; he confronts the inner-child nonsense in me by simply telling me to be a leader. Sometimes, it isn't what I want to hear, but it is most certainly what I need to hear, everyday. Jesus needs us to manage our emotions and be a leader of our own lives every day. Life is too short and precious to waste on a crazy emotional rollercoaster ride leading nowhere.

Think about this. Say, for instance, the average person is going to be on planet earth for one hundred years. Imagine if the Lord in his infinite wisdom decided to give you all one hundred years at once. There's your hundred years, go run about. You want to be a baby, be a baby. You want to be a 20-year-old, you can go be a 20 -year-old. You want to fast forward to being 50? You can be 50. Most of us have a remote control at home. It's used for entertainment. It's not something the Lord has given us to use on our own lives.

God gives us everyday on purpose as a perfect measure, and a perfect pace because he wants us to grow up!

God does not want us to press the rewind button on our lives, to go back to an era from which He has already delivered us. He does not want us to fast forward to a place where we think life will be easier and better, when He is in fact building us for that right now. Perhaps your bank balance is large today. Maybe next week it won't be large. Perhaps today your bank balance is small, but maybe next week He wants it to be large. We have today, only this day, to respond to God.

It's not helpful to always be thinking back, hoping back, looking back, and praying back. It is also not helpful to be always wishing "ahead", running ahead, pushing ahead, and trying to fast-forward ahead. We will not be ready for our future if we don't embrace our present, everyday.

#gone

"If only we could realize while we are yet mortals, that day by day we are building for eternity, how different our lives in many ways would be! Every gentle word, every generous thought, every unselfish deed, will become a pillar of eternal beauty in the life to come. We cannot be selfish and unloving in one life and generous and loving in the next. The two lives are too closely blended - one but a continuation of the other."[9]

Rebecca Ruter Springer
My Dream of Heaven

Our earth-life is God's perfect measure and we don't have a day to waste. We will not be ready if we do not live today. Perhaps all of your friends are married or getting married and you want to skip forward to that day in your own life. God has no desire to hold back anything good from us. God uses our everyday life to shape and prepare us. Our everyday life is His perfect measure and we do not have a day to waste. My hope for you is to find yourself positioned in the arms of your loving Heavenly Father and allow the full weight of your life to shift to His capable, strong, and caring arms, everyday.

My father was a fire fighter in the New South Wales Fire Brigade in Sydney Australia for 36 years. My earliest memories of my Dad are of him in his uniform kissing my Mum and us kids goodbye before going to work, and then kissing my Mum and us kids hello upon his arrival home from work.

My Dad was, and still is, a brave man. He is an amazing real life hero. What makes my Dad brave aren't all the wild and wonderful stories he loves to tell about those very many years of dangerous adventure as a fire fighter. What makes my Dad the brave hero that he is to me is his commitment to life, to my Mum, to us kids and to our family. Brave is simply this: commitment in plain clothes. My Dad, by the faithful example of his everyday life, inspired me to make the most of my life. As you recognize your life's purpose and see it in the light of eternity, do your best to work diligently, productively, fruitfully, but all from a place of rest. My prayer for you today is that you would know what it is to live a new life, free of the deadweight of your old life, of your own efforts, and of striving, everyday.

There is freedom in living GONE, everyday.

#gone

FAITHFULNESS

1. Show up

2. Show up on time

3. Show up on time with a great attitude

4. Show up on time with a great attitude EVERYDAY

5. Show up on time with a great attitude EVERYDAY and get something done.

John Siebeling

#pray

Father, thank you for your Word. Thank you Lord God for giving me a revelation; understanding of what it means to be gone in your arms. Father, I do not have to keep fighting my own way, at my own pace. I don't need to keep fighting the battles - you just want me to relax. Thank You, Father God, for my family. Lord, I know that there are always things going on. There are always health and financial concerns, and relationship problems, and I want to thank you, Father God, from that position of being gone in your arms, that there is an amazing relationship I can have. I want to leave the weight of all of it behind. And I pray, Lord God, for the chains to break today from that weight, that I would know the responsibility, but not feel that weight, Father. In Jesus' Name I pray!

Amen.

ordinary

of no special quality or interest; unexceptional; mediocre; plain;
undistinguished; somewhat inferior or below average

#anonymous

Jesus' hidden years ... and yours

"Our desire to 'be like Jesus' contains several exemption clauses, not the least of which are Jesus' hidden years, desert experiences, temptations, tortures, and crucifixion. We will pass on those, thank you. What we are most definitely interested in, however, is Jesus' character and authority. How we long to see His character and authority transform this broken world through our lives! But Jesus' character and authority are not isolated entities. They are not disconnected commodities we can purchase at a discount. Jesus' character and authority come with Jesus' life, 90 percent of which was lived in quiet anonymity. 'What would Jesus do!' we ask sincerely [in word and song on t-shirts and bracelets]. Well, for starters, He embraced a life of hiddenness..."[10]

Alicia Britt Chole
Anonymous

GONE is a revelation.

When we lay down our lives for the Lord, we are the beneficiaries. That means we are the ones who are designed to receive from this transaction. When we lay down our lives we are the ones who gain from it. How amazing that in our abandon, in our surrender, in our position of being GONE, we are the ones to gain! And that is how God designed it. We win in life when we surrender to God. It's very different from a dog-eat-dog world that demands every man or woman for him or herself.

This Kingdom principle is so contrary to the principles of the world we live in where surrender is an admission of defeat. To think you and I could benefit from being completely surrendered to our Creator God is a completely foreign concept to most people, and if you haven't read your Bible, you might believe you can only "lose" by giving your life away. In God's Kingdom, however, surrender is not defeat, but victorious freedom.

GONE is the moment of surrender. Sometimes our resistance to surrendering completely is the fear of the unknown, "What happens if I let myself go? What happens if I actually lay down my life? What happens if I fall asleep in the arms of God and I wake up alive to who I am? What happens when I am truly and utterly GONE?"

The truth is that when we are completely abandoned, when we are completely trusting, when we are completely at peace, the natural weight of our lives is transferred to our Supernatural God. When this happens, the every day, ordinary aspects of our lives will take on extraordinary qualities and we will start to live according to the principles of God's Kingdom rather than the principles of this earth-life world.

One Sunday, our daughter London was not feeling well. I kept her home from school the following day and by the next afternoon she announced that she was bored! "Ha!" I thought to myself, "bored means you're well again and ready to go back to school!"

#biblesays

"To find your life, you must lose your life – and whoever loses his life for My sake will find it."

matthew chapter ten verse thirty-nine

the voice

#gone

"If your everyday life seems poor, don't blame it; blame yourself; admit to yourself that you are not enough of a poet to call forth its riches; because for the Creator there is no poverty and no indifferent place."[1]

Rainer Maria Rilke

#gone

This is our EVERYDAY mandate:

1. Dedicate ourselves to God.

2. Humble ourselves before God.

3. Be faithful to God.

4. Use our spiritual gifts for God.

5. Stay at our posts as directed by God.

I pray that the Lord will give me a growing revelation of what it means to be GONE, and I pray the same for you. I encourage you to ask God to open your eyes to all of the amazing ways He can take this ordinary life you "think" you have and turn it into something extraordinary for His purpose.

Often, what we are going through in our life will determine our outlook in life. When we are not well, all we can think about is the day that we'll be healthy. When we are healthy, it is so easy for us to forget the power of everyday well-being. We can treat an amazing, health-filled day like it's just another ordinary day. We may even find ourselves saying, "I'm bored"! We should never use those words. Everyday is a gift from God for God. We need to make the most of our everyday from Him, for Him.

Perhaps you feel as though you are just an ordinary person, who grew up in an ordinary family, in an ordinary house, with ordinary grades, followed by an ordinary job, an ordinary wife with ordinary kids. My prayer is that God would give you a revelation of what it means to be GONE and He will illuminate your imagination to the amazing opportunities awaiting your everyday ordinary life. Your ordinary life is about to become extraordinary.

Our ordinary life becomes our extraordinary life when we:

1. Give all that we are   -   Talent
2. Give all that we have   -   Treasure
3. Give all we can do   -   Time

Give all that we are, give all that we have, give all that we do. I love that God asks the same thing from everyone, in every walk of life. He doesn't ask more from the type A personalities than everyone else. He doesn't want more or less of us based on gender, personality, home life, or socio-economic background. God makes it simple: He wants all of our lives from all of us. I don't know about you – but I can't do this in my own strength.

#gone

"Believers are to dedicate themselves to God. To be humble, and faithfully to use their spiritual gifts, in their respective stations. He entreated the Romans, as his brethren in Christ, by the mercies of God, to present their bodies as a living sacrifice to Him. This is a powerful appeal. We receive from the Lord every day the fruits of his mercy. Let us render ourselves; all we are, all we have, all we can do: and after all, what return is it for such very rich receivings? It is acceptable to God: a reasonable service, which we are able and ready to give a reason for, and which we understand."[2]

Matthew Henry Commentary
romans chapter twelve verses one and two

Our own selfishness will challenge our decision on every single one of these things. Our "self" will want to measure these things. Our "self" will want to allocate. Our "self" will want to deliberate. Our "self" will want to have a committee meeting about any of these things at any given time. The only way you can give all that you are, all that you have, and all you can do – is from a position of GONE. GONE is a position of Spirit-empowered grace, where "self" does not have the final say.

Maybe life has been a struggle. Maybe you have sensed God call you to serve Him and you are finding it a struggle and frustration. This is most likely because your spirit is willing but your "self" is not. Maybe that ultimate moment of surrender hasn't happened yet. We cannot possibly give all that we have, all that we are, and all that we can do from our un-surrendered "self." You will have all out war within your "self." When a man and woman fall in love and decide to get married, it can be a very beautiful thing. A potential problem occurs when one partner only gives themselves partially to the other. Partial commitment is no real commitment at all. We should determine to be "all or nothing" in our decision. As for me, I choose surrender. I choose to be GONE.

When it comes to marriage and family and other important relationships and commitments, I have found it easier, not harder, to be there for people, from a position of GONE. When I am at peace with my Maker and myself, I am a nicer person with a much bigger capacity. When I give of myself from a place of GONE, I don't experience loss, but I do experience gain. We can try to give all of our talent, all of our treasure and all of our time to various people, projects and things, but we will find ourselves worn thin and burnt out. Our marriage is important, our kids are important, our parents are important, our job is important. Then there are sports, hobbies, demanding friends, relatives and social media networks. Everyone and everything demands a piece of us and our ordinary life, everyday.

The wisest way to live is to commit your life and your ways to God everyday. When we choose to give all that we are – our talent, give all that we have – our treasure, and give all we can do – our time, to God on purpose for His purpose, He enlarges our lives, and builds character and capacity in us for more than we could ever do in our own strength.

We can give all that we are, our time, our talent, our treasure to our job, and at the end of it – guess what – you'll retire. Or you might be fired. Remember, we can give all that we are to our kids, and that is noble, and that is important, but they are not God, and we need to remember that. We can give all that we are to our hobbies or to a favorite sport. We can give all that we are to our demanding relatives. What would happen if you told your non-religious relatives or your religious relatives that you want to give all that you are, all that you have, and all that you can do to God? They might try to talk you out of it, especially the religious ones. They will tell you to be measured. They may try to give you all kinds of advice about you needing to be more "balanced." Of course, if you're trying to live life in your own strength, you will constantly feel that you need to find balance in your life. But when you live life from a position of GONE, it helps simplify life. Our surrendered life is a brand new life and it is a custom-fit, Kingdom first life.

God created us for GONE, and every other way we live is actually a poor imitation compared to a GONE life with God. In the GONE life we experience the extraordinary friendship and presence of God in our ordinary lives. Others may look at our lives and say we should measure what we give God of our time, talent, and treasure. Or if we are afraid to surrender, we try to measure in our own strength how much of our time, talent, and treasure we will give to God. When we do this we are really measuring how much of God we will allow into those areas of our lives. I don't know about you, but it doesn't make sense to try and use measure with an immeasurable God.

#biblesays

"But seek [aim at and strive after] first of all His Kingdom and His righteousness [His way of doing and being right], and then all these things taken together will be given you besides."

matthew chapter six verse thirty-three
amplified version

God created us for GONE and GONE is where we will be most ourselves, most at peace, most alive, no matter what others or our fears may suggest.

We can give everything that we have and all that we are to our hobbies, to worthy causes, to family and friends who need us, but we find that they always need more from us. They need more love, or more time. It's the never-ending story. Or we can give all that we are, all that we have and all that we can do, to God and His purpose.

God understands that all of these things are important. He understands our children are important, our husbands are important, our families are important. Our hobbies are even important to God. God loves us! If we understand "first" and "and then," we understand that the ultimate moment of surrender is when we allow the Lord to reprioritize our life.

Sometimes people think that if they are going to give their life away to Jesus, they can't give it away to anything or anyone else. Matthew 6:33 reminds us that "these things taken together" will be given to you, but not only that! The verse also says that these things will be given to you "besides." Apparently, there is a bonus that comes in allowing the Lord to reprioritize our lives.

So what are all these things? They are ordinary things. They are the ordinary things we know we need – that God knows we need, and He is ready and very well prepared to give us. Our primary focus should be heaven as our end, and whole-heartedness as our way there. We should seek the comforts of the Kingdom. We should aim our focus at the Kingdom of Heaven. We should press thoughtfully toward Heaven. We should prefer the blessings of Heaven over the offerings of earth. All the concerns of this life should be made subordinate to those of the life to come. We should seek the things of Christ more than our own desires. In a competing moment, we should remember what is most important.

A competing moment is an opportunity for you to discover if you are truly surrendered or not. Competing moments will come your way, and then you recognize that your choice will be a fruit of surrender – or not. If ever a competing moment comes, we should remember what is important.

Competing moments occur when people try to pull us in one direction, when we know we are right on course in another. Competing moments happen when our calendar represents our GONE life and all kinds of other events vie for attention. Competing moments are with us everyday in our ordinary decision-making. A GONE life is a flexible life, making everything work together so that there is harmony in everything we do. What should be inflexible in our life is our posture of GONE.

We should seek the Kingdom of God early in our day and early in our years. The sooner we seek God and His Kingdom, the sooner true wisdom abounds in our life. Let our waking thoughts be of God. Let our everyday, ordinary lives be yielded to God. Let this be our everyday, ordinary custom: do first what is most important, most needed, most fruitful, and let God, Who is the First, have the first of us.

Does God have the first of you? Do you give Him the leftovers at the end of the day? Is He in your waking thoughts? Is He the focus of your day because of your relationship with Him? Religious duties are very different from personal relationship. When we walk in a personal relationship with our Maker, we don't have to perform religious duties to please Him or appease Him.

The Bible teaches us about the first fruits and the leftovers in the story of Cain and Abel. This story in Genesis 4, tells of both brothers bringing their offerings to the Lord. Cain's brought his leftovers, while Abel's brought his prime, first fruits selection. Abel's offering was acceptable to the Father because it was his best. Do we give God our best or do we present to him what is left over?

#gone

"The best way to be comfortably provided for in this world, is to be most intent upon another world!"[3]

Matthew Henry Commentary
matthew chapter six verse thirty-three

It should be our life's greatest joy to give all that we are – our talent; all that we have – our treasure; and all that we can do – our time, to God for His purpose. After all, this is why we were created.

God's gracious promise is annexed as, "all these things." Do you know what an annex is? Have you ever been camping in a caravan? Not in a luxurious RV, but a caravan or trailer? Always hope that if you go camping in a caravan, there is an annex. The annex is the attached space. It is not part of the vehicle, but is actually an attached shade space. God literally annexes our life. He attaches a bonus to our life that we need to recognize literally comes with us putting His kingdom first. God's gracious promise is annexed to us as "all these things."

What are all "these things?" They are ordinary support for our everyday lives. We don't need to feel anxious and worry so that they become our prime focus. Do we need somewhere to live? Yes. Do we need something to eat? Yes. God's literal promise to us is that when we take care of His business, He promises to take care of our business.

If I could choose a business partner, whom would I choose? Me or God? Would I choose myself as my business partner, or would I choose God Almighty? Literally, this is the promise: when we take care of His business, He promises, annexes, and gives us bonuses to take care of ours. God's promise to us is to provide for us, over and above what we need. This is a revelation. It requires us to understand this is truth and we need to trust truth. When we seek His Kingdom first, we shall have what we seek – His Kingdom!

Have you ever thought about that? "Seek first the Kingdom" – what does that actually mean? When we seek something, we do so with an expectation to find something. Therefore when we seek the Kingdom first, we shall have what we seek. This is a complete game changer. If you understand this, you receive keys to somewhere you didn't have keys to before. You get keys to the Kingdom. Would you like to get out of that bind you're in? Would you like to have a different life? Would you like to stop feeling you're in a poverty cycle? Would you like to stop being in relational dysfunction? You need keys to a better place.

Would you like to trade in your ordinary life for His extraordinary Kingdom? The benefits are amazing! When we enter into Kingdom life, we are transformed from commoner to royalty. Royalty is the highest possible class of life and it is offered to those who have chosen to surrender their ordinary life in exchange for His extraordinary life. Earth-life royals transcend class, since their position is not dependent on economic status. When we surrender our lives, the exchange is miraculous. We inherit the Kingdom. When we seek His Kingdom first, we shall have what we seek. It gives our King great pleasure to give us His Kingdom. There is nothing ordinary about the King or His Kingdom, yet He truly wants us to make the exchange of our ordinary for His Kingdom. When we inherit the Kingdom of God, we are transformed from ordinary to extraordinary.

The concept of what a kingdom truly is and all it entails is quite a leap for those who didn't grow up in a land with a history of monarchy. Kings and queens, princes and princesses seem almost like something out of a fairy tale. I caught a glimpse of what living in a kingdom might be like when I was in London England one summer, visiting the Tower of London seeing the crown jewels. I was looking for the Tower, expecting to see a skyscraper, but was surprised to find the crown jewels were contained in an old stone building just two stories high! The building wasn't at all what I had expected, but the crown jewels inside gave it all the value in the world. Once inside, visitors weren't even able to stand in front of the crown jewels. They had to be viewed from a distance as visitors moved slowly past them on a conveyor belt.

The realization of how precious and rare the treasures of the kingdom were opened my eyes in a new way to the value of the kingdom treasures in each of us. Yes they are housed in humble, unimpressive vessels; "jars of clay." as the apostle Paul calls our earthly bodies. But the presence of the Kingdom treasures we carry within us add immense value to the ordinary lives we lead! Try one day to go and see a castle. Do whatever you need to do to expand your understanding of Kingdom life. We need to understand the Kingdom is actually amazing and desirable; otherwise, what are we seeking? It's not simply about getting to heaven. Kingdom-mindedness brings Kingdom to earth for us. We should be more thoughtful and consumed about the things that are unseen [the eternal] and less thoughtful about the seen [the temporal]. Our everyday, ordinary lives are highly valued by God and should be highly valued by us. Popular culture seems to scorn the ordinary and does everything possible to avoid association with it. There is something we're sold – some sort of lie – where we have to trade in our ordinary life for something else here on earth.

The only thing that the Bible tells us to trade in for our earth-life is the Kingdom life. Popular culture tells us, when life seems boring or ordinary to go and fill the void with whatever makes us feel good. Popular culture tells us that if we change ourselves to be like another person we will find ourselves really happy. We buy into the lie that ordinary is not cool – so we must become somebody else on earth. Ordinary is powerful in the right hands. It's sad when people try to fix things in a temporal way, thinking their life will change. When we seek the Kingdom first, it makes sense of our ordinary. It is the only exchange that God asks of us.

Ordinary is: average, common, commonplace, cut-and-dry, everyday, garden-variety, normal, routine, run-of-the-mill, standard, unexceptional, unremarkable, usual, regular, typical, familiar, homely, plain, plain-Jane, customary, insignificant, trivial, unimportant; frequent, habitual; expected, predictable. Our ordinary life in God's hands becomes our extraordinary life.

I live in a very beautiful part of the world – Orange County in Southern California. My kids go to school in a very beautiful part of the world, and all of the moms are very beautiful. They seem from the outside to have everything they could ever possibly want, and yet I hear them describe their lives using all those words above for "ordinary." In truth, there is absolutely nothing ordinary about their lives. The homes, the cars, the yachts, the shopping, the people and the pets – everything is extraordinary according to even the world's standards! However, within every human soul is a longing for meaning beyond what this earth-life could ever satisfy. Some try to fulfill their lives by doing whatever they want; buying more, fixing more, changing more, but they still have an ordinary life unless they are fulfilling the destiny dream purpose of their lives. The only way to get an extraordinary life is to exchange it with the Lord for His Kingdom.

All of the above in God's hands becomes our extraordinary life! When we think about the word ordinary, it comes with all of those descriptive words. None of us want ordinary just for the sake of ordinary, but if I hand God my ordinary, He can transform it into extraordinary. Kingdom favor is the evidence of the Kingdom of God in our lives!

When living a fully surrendered life we can look forward to extraordinary Kingdom benefits.

1. Surprising, Uncommon and Unusual KINGDOM Favor
   Surprising everyone because they attempted to change their ordinary to extraordinary by buying something, or doing something, or meeting someone, or climbing something, and all you did was make a pure Kingdom exchange. You prayed, "Father, I am GONE. I surrender all." Uncommon and unusual Kingdom favor is when you experience something amazing that isn't experienced by the majority of humanity. It is when we

surrender our ordinary common life to God that we experience extraordinary and uncommon favor.

2. Special and "Beyond" KINGDOM Favor
When it seems as though you are God's special favorite. Yes you are! Every single one of us is, and we should live as such. God is able to make us feel special when we live surrendered to His love. You may also experience God's favor that could be described as being "above and beyond." There is a certain expectation you are going to live a blessed life as a Christian, a certain expectation that if you are tithing there is going to be an open window over your life. There is a level of favor beyond expectation.

3. Rare and Remarkable KINGDOM Favor
This is favor that causes people to say, "That never happens!" or, "When does that ever happen?" It's just so rare! Have you ever experienced rare Kingdom favor? I have! If you haven't yet – you will! Seek first His Kingdom and all these things will be added to you. All these things are big and small, common and rare. Ask God to surprise you – ask Him to knock you off your feet with Kingdom favor. Perhaps you're thinking of things that have happened to you which have been very remarkable Kingdom favor. Or perhaps somebody you know has experienced remarkable Kingdom favor because they handed their ordinary life to an extraordinary God and so they experienced the extraordinary.

4. Noteworthy and Unprecedented KINGDOM Favor
You become history! You receive such favor that it puts you in a history book as your amazing story is recorded. You receive such an amazing blessing in your life no one has ever even heard of it before – you're the first.

#gone

"We are halfhearted creatures, fooling about with drink and sex and ambition when infinite joy is offered us, like an ignorant child who wants to go on making mud pies in a slum because he cannot imagine what is meant by the offer of a holiday at the sea."[4]

C.S. Lewis

5. Unimaginable KINGDOM Favor:
This is favor that is outside of anything you could have thought or dreamed of in your wildest imagination. This is incomprehensible favor that may not have been seen or heard before. Our human mind can only dream so far and then God blows us away by doing the unimaginable for us.

One thing we clearly need to understand is that all this Kingdom favor is for our benefit so that we can be a benefit to others. We must always remember that we are blessed to be a blessing. My hope is that this revelation of the surrender of our ordinary lives will undo us, that it will unravel all of our limited thinking, that it will challenge our misguided belief systems. Let us understand: when we seek first the Kingdom, we get what we seek. This is what we are going to get because this is what we are seeking first.

God does not call us to be extraordinary by any means. He does not set a benchmark like we might set for ourselves. He does not set a benchmark that other people would create for us. He says, "Give me your ordinary, then watch what I will do." That's a relief. I'm not that brilliant, God knows. Some of us work so hard on our brilliance. We should work harder on our surrender.

In fact, it's through Him that our ordinary lives become extraordinary. When God calls us, He calls us to live our everyday ordinary lives. Some of us don't pick up the call because we're too busy getting ready for a big opportunity.

When God calls us, we need to answer the call. How quick are we to respond to the call? What is the call? We don't need to be confused about the call. In this context, the call is surrender. Will you need to take three days to pray about it when Jesus is calling you? To whom would you be praying? Jesus Himself is the One Who is calling you! We don't need to over think it or over-spiritualize it.

#gone

"God can do anything, you know—far more than you could ever imagine or guess or request in your wildest dreams! He does it not by pushing us around but by working within us, his Spirit deeply and gently within us."

ephesians three verse twenty

the message

When the Lord is calling you to surrender – surrender! The quicker you do it, the less painful it is.

Jesus' disciples were willing to leave their ordinary life behind only to inherit a life rich with purpose. I'm sure the disciples didn't wake up everyday and say, "Yay!" I'm sure they woke up everyday and said "hard work!" when it came to their ordinary life. What is powerful to note is that the disciples left at once. They did not stop to think they were too ordinary – or too extraordinary – for service. When we seek the Kingdom, we receive the Kingdom. One of the reasons that we stop and hold back is we aren't sure we're worthy of service. The disciples also didn't stop to consider their ordinary life as unfit for use in Kingdom life. Their "ordinary" wasn't too small for Jesus to use, neither was it too valuable.

Many truly love their ordinary life of trying to make it on their own. Who would want an ordinary life instead of an extraordinary Kingdom life? No one would want ordinary over extraordinary, if they understood the difference! Once we understand something, we have an opportunity to change our lives. Understanding can become conviction. Conviction then becomes an amazing, unstoppable force in our lives. On those mornings when you wake up and it's difficult, and you feel like you're going through the motions, you need to seek the Kingdom and receive the Kingdom. We need to seek God's Kingdom first every day, for we desperately need what God offers the subjects of His Kingdom each day. When we lay our ordinary lives down and inherit a life in Christ – we become anything but ordinary. We become extraordinary.

Spending relational time with God by praying and reading your Bible and focusing your everyday ordinary purpose in Him, will cause you to stand out from the crowd, and will take your life from ordinary to extraordinary! After Moses spent time with God, his face visibly glowed so much that he had to wear a veil to cover himself while around the rest of the community; it was too much for them to bear.

#biblesays

"One day as Jesus was walking along the shore of the Sea of Galilee, he saw two brothers—Simon, also called Peter, and Andrew—throwing a net into the water, for they fished for a living. Jesus called out to them, 'Come, follow me, and I will show you how to fish for people!' And they left their nets at once and followed him. A little farther up the shore he saw two other brothers, James and John, sitting in a boat with their father, Zebedee, repairing their nets. And he called them to come, too. They immediately followed him, leaving the boat and their father behind."

matthew chapter four verses eighteen to twenty-two
new living translation

Moses stood out from the crowd because he had been in the presence of God.

The Sermon on the Mount is an amazing passage of scripture about the disciples who were with Jesus. Jesus pulled them aside after a hectic season of ministry. They had been with the crowds, and now it was time for them to understand the Kingdom.

The Kingdom of God seems upside-down to the crowds, those who don't understand it. But those of us who have come to understand and love the Kingdom, know that it is right-side up.

When the crowd says, "First one to finish line wins," the Kingdom says, "Truly the first will be last and the last will be first."

When the crowd says, "All publicity is good publicity. Do whatever it takes to get noticed!" the Kingdom says, "Truly those who seem least now will be those who are most then."

When the crowd says, "He who dies with the most toys wins," the Kingdom says, "Truly those who give, will be those who receive."

God is saying to us all, "You need to understand the Kingdom. You have just been with the crowds, now you need to understand the Kingdom." It is time for us to learn and value Kingdom life above the ways of the crowd.

We can see our ordinary lives become extraordinary as we believe that God can and will grant us the desires of our heart. God did not put that dream in your heart to frustrate you. He put that dream in your heart to see it come to life, in your lifetime. If He said it, He will complete it, and He will use your everyday lives to bring your dreams to pass. It starts with valuing the ordinary days of your life.

Ordinary becomes extraordinary through creativity.

God created us to be creative. We are created in the image of a creative God. We are given the opportunity to present the gospel to people in ways that weren't even possible decades ago. The challenge is now that people have so many options, that living for Jesus has become "an ordinary option" rather than "our best option."

#biblesays

"One day as He saw the crowds gathering, Jesus went up on the mountainside and sat down. His disciples gathered around him, and He began to teach them. "God blesses those who are poor and realize their need for Him, for the Kingdom of Heaven is theirs. God blesses those who mourn, for they will be comforted. God blesses those who are humble, for they will inherit the whole earth. God blesses those who hunger and thirst for justice, for they will be satisfied. God blesses those who are merciful, for they will be shown mercy. God blesses those whose hearts are pure, for they will see God. God blesses those who work for peace, for they will be called the children of God. God blesses those who are persecuted for doing right, for the Kingdom of Heaven is theirs. God blesses you when people mock you and persecute you and lie about you and say all sorts of evil things against you because you are my followers. Be happy about it! Be very glad! For a great reward awaits you in Heaven. And remember, the ancient prophets were persecuted in the same way."

matthew chapter five verses one to twelve
new international version

#gone

CREATIVITY

"To cause to come into being, as something unique that would not naturally evolve or that is not made by ordinary processes; to evolve from one's own thought or imagination, as a work of art or an invention; to form, fashion, shape, hone, present."

the dictionary

The creative war is for both our attention and our affection. We can't keep trying to outdo ourselves or outdo the world around us. We just need to stay focused on Jesus, His message, His mandate and His methods. We just need to stay focused on bringing heaven to earth. We were not born to build the latest "Kingdom brand." We were born to know Jesus and to make Him known. No competition, no comparison. Our greatest commitment should be to knowing Jesus and making Him known, but we can't make someone known that we don't know ourselves. Let's make knowing Jesus our first priority so that we can make Him known. Whatever or whomever we love, we will promote.

The message of Jesus will never tire or go out of fashion. There is nothing new under the sun but Jesus and His gospel is forever alive and fresh! Our concern is not to be fashionable, but to remain faithful with our everyday ordinary lives.

Fashion is all about popularity, how we dress, what ornaments we own, how we behave, our style, manner, way, our shape, mold, model, make, swag. Ultimately our role is not to be the "fashionistas" of God's Kingdom; to come up with all the creative ideas. Rather we need to harness and tap into the creativity of our Creator for the sole purpose of making Him known. We ought to be leaders in creativity, not to make ourselves famous or to stand out, but so that when people cross paths with us in our everyday ordinary life, they will encounter something never seen, heard, or felt before. Our desire should be to present people with an experience likened to a taste of "Heaven on earth." God created us and we're created in the image of a creative God.

We have been created in the image and likeness of God. We have been created by God to create for God. Our "chronos" [earth time] needs to meet God's "kairos" [eternity time]. Our "kairos" is already created; we can and must tap into Heaven, into God's ideas.

#biblesays

"So God created human beings in His own image. In the image of God He created them; male and female He created them."

genesis chapter one verse twenty-seven

new living translation

#gone

"We have here the second part of the sixth day's work, the creation of man, which we are, in a special manner, concerned to take notice of, that we may know ourselves. Observe: that man was made last of all the creatures, that it might not be suspected that he had been, any way, a helper to God in the creation of the world: that question must be for ever humbling and mortifying to him..."[6]

Matthew Henry Commentary
genesis chapter one verse twenty-seven

Our ordinary life becomes extraordinary when we don't sell out for fashion and fads. Fashion comes and fashion goes. We cannot afford to become conformed to it. Fashion can be such a distraction, we must be careful not to lose our message in the midst of it.

We are encouraged, or rather, instructed in Romans 12:2 not to be conformed to this world [fashioned after and adapted to its external, superficial customs], but to be transformed and changed by the [entire] renewal of our minds [by its new ideals and its new attitude], so that we may prove [for ourselves] what is the good and acceptable and perfect will of God, even the thing which is good and acceptable and perfect [in His sight for us][5].

We have the mind of Christ. If we grasp this we can always be thinking about what matters most. What God thinks is more important than what we think. Our personal taste must give way to His greater purpose for our lives.

The life work of Jesus is beyond our creative comprehension. What we have to study of Him is all we need. Jesus kept His message simple; powerful but simple. Jesus kept His message simple. We need to keep it simple. He kept it inclusive. We need to keep it inclusive. He kept it real. We need to keep it real. He kept His focus. We need to keep our focus. Jesus believed the Words He said. We need to believe the Words He said. He kept His mission. We need to keep His mission.

And His mission was this: **Jesus gave His heart to God and people, and He used His talent, time and treasure – His whole life – to fulfill his purpose, everyday.** God gave us our time and talent and treasure, so that we can use it for Him. What does he want us to give Him? Our heart. If we give Him our heart and use those things for Him we'll have a happily-ever-after extraordinary life, everyday.

#biblesays

"Jesus also did many other things. If they were all written down, I suppose the whole world could not contain the books that would be written."

john chapter twenty-one verse twenty-five
new living translation

#gone

JESUS

"If it be asked why the gospels are not larger, why they did not make the New Testament history as copious and as long as the Old, it may be answered... It was not because they had exhausted their subject... Everything that Christ said and did was worth our notice... He never spoke an idle word, nor did an idle thing; he never spoke nor did anything mean, or little, or trifling, which is more than can be said of the wisest or best of men. His miracles were many, very many, of many kinds, and the same often repeated, as occasion offered. Every new miracle rendered the report of the former the more credible; and the multitude of them renders the whole report incontestable. When we speak of Christ, we have a copious subject before us; the reality exceeds the report. There were many other things, which were not written because there was no occasion for writing them... It was not possible to write all. It was possible for the Spirit to indite all, but morally impossible for the penmen to pen all. The world could not contain the books... It would be such a large and overgrown history as never was; such as would jostle out all other writings, and leave us no room for them. What volumes would be filled with Christ's prayers, had we the record of all those he made, when he continued all night in prayer to God, without any vain repetitions? ... It was not advisable to write much; for the world, in a moral sense, could not contain the books that should be written. Christ said not what he might have said to his disciples, because they were not able to bear it...; and for the same reason the evangelists wrote not what they might have written. All people's time would have been spent in reading, and other duties would thereby have been crowded out..."[7]

Matthew Henry Commentary

john chapter twenty-one verse twenty-five

#pray

Father, thank you in Jesus' name for your Word. Thank you for truth. Thank you, Father God, for understanding. Lord, as I seek your Kingdom, thank you that I can expect to receive what I seek – Your Kingdom. Thank you Lord that I don't need to be concerned or fret over the things of this earth. But as I aim for and strive after Your Kingdom, I understand You will meet all of those needs, that they are valid. Lord, help me embrace my moment of surrender. Father God, in this ultimate moment of surrender, allow me please to experience Kingdom favor. I let go of my old life and embrace all that You have for me. I love Your presence. Father, thank you for Your grace abounding in my life. Thank you for my ordinary life, every single day. In Jesus' Name I pray.

Amen.

#anonymous

Jesus' hidden years ... and yours

"What grows in that underestimated gap between God's calling and others' perceptions, between our true capabilities and our current realities? Most of us struggle if our dreams are delayed one year, let alone twenty! We find God's pauses perplexing. They seem to be a waste of our potential. When those pauses extend beyond what we can comprehend or explain [say, for instance, three days], we often spiral into self-doubt or second-guessing. But in anonymous seasons we must hold tightly to the truth that no doubt strengthened Jesus throughout his hidden years: Father God is neither 'care-less' nor 'cause-less' with how He spends our lives. When He calls a soul simultaneously to greatness and obscurity, the fruit – if we wait for it – can change the world."[8]

Alicia Britt Chole
Anonymous

3

sleeping

to take the rest afforded by a suspension of voluntary bodily functions; the
natural suspension, complete or partial, of consciousness; cease being awake

#biblesays

GOODNIGHT

"Don't worry about anything; instead, pray about everything. Tell God what you need, and thank him for all he has done. Then you will experience God's peace, which exceeds anything we can understand. His peace will guard your hearts and minds as you live in Christ Jesus."

philippians chapter four verses six and seven
new living translation

#biblesays

GOOD MORNING

"And now, dear brothers and sisters, one final thing. Fix your thoughts on what is true, and honorable, and right, and pure, and lovely, and admirable. Think about things that are excellent and worthy of praise. Keep putting into practice all you learned and received from me—everything you heard from me and saw me doing. Then the God of peace will be with you."

philippians chapter four verses eight and nine
new living translation

We have been created in the image of God, by God, for God.

With each new day, God has given us the opportunity to give Him our everyday life. When we give him all that we are, all that we have and all that we can do, every day, he takes our ordinary lives and makes them into extraordinary trophies of grace. When we seek Him and His Kingdom first, we get what we seek – His Kingdom. When we give him our ordinary lives, He makes our lives extraordinary.

Our everyday, ordinary lives consist of our waking hours and sleeping hours. It's easy to think of our everyday, ordinary lives in the context of daylight hours, but what about our sleep? Our sleep patterns change over the course of our lives. I can recall a few seasons in my life that were remarkably different from each other, starting with my teenage years. Going to bed very late [or very early in the morning] and waking up very late [or very early in the afternoon].

Then as an adult and becoming a mother, everything changed. Everyone said over and over, "Make sure you get plenty of sleep now, because..." Yes, I knew. My life was about to change forever. And then I had twins! They were actually great sleepers from just a few weeks old, but nevertheless, my life and my sleep were no longer my own.

My youngest daughter, London, was a dream sleeper until she reached the age of three. We had traveled with her many times from Los Angeles to Sydney and she coped well with the time changes each trip. London had slept twelve to fourteen hours every night without waking, for her first three years. Then, after one trip to Sydney, we came home to California and she just wouldn't sleep. My husband Jonathan and I spent the next twelve months waking every night trying to settle her back to sleep, and then eventually bringing her into our bed so we could all get some sleep. This was something we vowed that we would never do.

Sleep can make us or break us.

#biblesays

"I lie awake thinking of you, meditating on you through the night."

psalm chapter sixty-three verse six
new living translation

#gone

"When you have accomplished your daily tasks, go to sleep in peace. God is awake."[1]

Victor Hugo

As a teenager, I can remember being woken up in the early afternoon by my grandmother and being annoyed about it because at that time I had no concept at all of "go to bed early, wake up early," or "go to bed moderately, wake up moderately." I would wake up at sometime between one o' clock and three o' clock in the afternoon because one o' clock to three o' clock in the morning was when I went to bed. It really didn't matter to me, and I didn't care, because I wasn't thinking about the loss of a day - I wasn't thinking about what I could be doing with that time. I used to be obsessed about getting enough sleep, and now I'm obsessed with making the most of every moment of my everyday.

You grow up and become an adult, find a husband, have a baby, and then there's that sound, "Waaahhh!" The sound of a crying baby is an in built alarm for us to care. That sound reminds us to wake up and feed the baby. It reminds us to wake up and look after the baby. That alarm is inside all of us – whether you have had natural children or not, God has wired you to nurture. God has wired you to wake up and care, wake up and feed, wake up and do something for someone else. The Bible says that He gives His beloved sleep. Having a child wake us up at night is a legitimate wake-up call. When we are waking up in the middle of the night because of worry, stress, workload, and all the wrong reasons, we need to address those things so that so we can sleep in heavenly peace, the way we were created to sleep.

Once, I was away on a ministry speaking engagement on the East Coast. I usually set two alarms for myself each morning so that I'm never late - I don't like to be late and I don't like to rush unnecessarily. I can do late and I can do rush – but I choose not to. And as a general rule, I like to over-prepare. I was booked to fly home to the West Coast on a flight that was scheduled to depart at 6.30am. That meant I had a 1.00am wake up call in West Coast time to get up. I honestly don't know what I was thinking when I booked a flight with a departure time of that hour! I typically like to have an hour and a half in the morning to get ready. I don't spend all that time doing my hair and my face, which only takes about 10-15 minutes. The rest of that time is me being able to think, being able to consider my day, having at least two cups of tea and reading my Bible, doing cardio and everything else I may want to do. So the night before my flight home, I set my alarm for 3.45am, and I set another alarm for 4.00am. [I don't trust my snooze button in case my finger slips in the morning]. Each day I set two separate alarms. My phone alarm goes off twice and I get two double snoozes, which drives my husband crazy!

The morning of my flight home, I was so concerned that I might not wake up at the right time, that I woke up at 3.40am, which was five minutes before my first alarm was due to go off. I got up, went to the restroom and put the kettle on – because, for me, tea is very important. And because I knew I had that other alarm set to go off at 4.00am, I turned off the first snooze. I went back to bed, put my head down on the pillow – next thing I knew there was knock, knock, knock at my door. It was suddenly eight minutes past 5.00am! The driver was waiting downstairs. My friends who were traveling with me just stood there looking at me. I was still standing at the door, not moving. My friends had never seen me that rattled, ever. Thankfully, I was packed and ready. I don't go to sleep with my clothes still folded in the dresser – that's not my style. Everything was packed and ready – except me! I got ready in a hurry though! I did manage a cup of tea, and I was downstairs within six minutes. BOOM, done. I had no makeup on and I just shook out my hair. When I arrived in Dallas, I made myself into a real Texan when I applied my makeup and fixed my hair.

There is some sleep that's helpful, and some sleep that's unhelpful, like over-sleeping an alarm. I looked back at the alarm later and it was still blue. That means it never went off. So now I set three alarms. My husband Jonathan is so happy about that.

#gone

"I am an old man and have known a great many troubles, but most of them have never happened."[2]

Mark Twain

My concept when it comes to sleep involves bookends. We go to sleep in order to wake up. When we go to sleep we should have words that frame our thoughts. We can choose to go to sleep saying, "Don't worry about anything, pray about everything." Then, when we wake up in the morning we can choose to think good thoughts. The Bible gives us wonderful bookends to live by and to sleep by.

Our sleeping is about our awakening. Our goodnight is all about our good morning. Our night is about our day. If we don't make it our habit to give God our drama as we're going to sleep, we'll go to sleep with our drama and wake up with it. You simply cannot wake up thinking about good things if you still have all that drama whirring away in your heart and mind. We need to get rid of it before we go to sleep if we want to have a good night and a good morning.

GOOD NIGHT!
Don't worry about anything, but pray about everything.

GOOD MORNING!
Think good thoughts today.

Perhaps you need a little more sleep, but what happens when you wake up, tossing and turning, worrying and panicking, thinking and over-thinking? After all, nights can be so dark.

It was a balmy September morning when I arrived downstairs to prepare for "Breakky [Breakfast] Club." I opened the laundry room door to drop some washing in the tub, to find that the door leading to outside was slightly ajar. Closing and locking it, I didn't think anything more of it at the time. Beau arrived downstairs that Tuesday morning to ask me why his phone was in the upstairs hallway with the alarm going off. I didn't have an explanation for him, only to say that I was sure he must have dropped it. He assured me he hadn't. The morning moved on. That evening I had been on a walk with my Mum who was visiting from Australia at the time. We enjoyed the serenity of our surroundings and had spoken about what a lovely neighborhood it was. That night we all went to bed and fell asleep.

At approximately 4.00am I was awoken by a presence in our room – a physical presence. I looked over to Jonathan's side of the bed and was about to ask him to please come back to bed. I was about to suggest that whatever was so important to be dealing with then, could wait until the morning, until I sat up and realized Jonathan was still fast asleep in our bed, and the man standing two inches from him was an intruder. London was sleeping in between us that evening as she had been waking in the night and couldn't get back to sleep, so I was very grateful I knew where she was when this stranger appeared. I quickly slinked down under the covers, completely afraid of what this man would do. He walked down past Jonathan's side of the bed, across the end of our bed and towards the door. When he was escaping is when I woke Jonathan to let him know there was someone in our room! He took longer than usual to stir. [I still to this day cannot believe that Jonathan didn't wake up with a stranger present in our room!]

Jonathan woke up with a fright and flew down the stairs. He checked every door and every window, and came back upstairs drawing a blank. We both figured it must have been a dream, but I wasn't asleep when it happened. We sat there in bed for hours trying to work out what had happened. We called the police in the morning, figuring that we needed to do something. The police came and investigated everything for hours. The police came to the conclusion that it might have been my imagination. I was willing to accept that the police thought I was crazy, until Beau reminded me about his phone, and I remembered the outside door from the laundry being ajar. And we found a cut in the screen of the same door that would have been all an intruder needed to put their hand in and unlock the door.

We decided to pursue the case. A neighbor's son arrived at our home a few days later with a similar story. That was enough for us to know what broke our sleep that night was very, very real. The intruder struck one more time in our neighborhood and this time, the homeowner tackled him in the hallway. The young man escaped but the victim managed to remember his appearance in detail.

The police arrived at my home with a photo identification line up. I was asked to choose two men out of twelve possibilities. If I could choose one and it was the identified intruder, they would prosecute him for home invasion. If I could choose two men and he was one of them, then they would prosecute him for the crime he committed where he was caught and tackled by the victim. I managed to choose two. I was unable to choose one, as there were two men who had identical haircuts and body frames, and it was dark so I couldn't see facial features. The young man received community service hours for his crimes. I received a season of very disturbed sleep as the movie reel of that fateful night played over and over in my head for the next twelve months.

Sometimes, like I did after our break-in, we lose sleep over something that has happened to us in the past. Other times we lose sleep over something we fear might happen. I lost sleep because I feared such a break-in might happen again. It was hard to keep that little seed of "what if" from bearing the fruit of fearful sleeplessness each night. Have you ever had just one little thought turn into an entire scenario? Over-thinking our problems will lead us down a road of negativity. We need to have a good night's sleep. If you're prone to worried thoughts at bedtime, make it a point to memorize this verse: "Don't worry about anything but pray about everything." When we put this verse into practice, then we can simply say, "GOOD NIGHT!"

We worry about more than we will ever have to live.

"Worry does not empty tomorrow of its sorrow, it empties today of its strength."[3]

Corrie Ten Boom

#biblesays

"I look up to the mountains; does my strength come from mountains? No, my strength comes from God, who made heaven, and earth, and mountains. He won't let you stumble, your Guardian God won't fall asleep. Not on your life! Israel's Guardian will never doze or sleep. God's your Guardian, right at your side to protect you - Shielding you from sunstroke, sheltering you from moonstroke. God guards you from every evil, he guards your very life. He guards you when you leave and when you return, he guards you now, He guards you always."

psalm chapter one hundred and twenty-one verses one to eight the message

#gone

10 Benefits of Sleep

1. Sleep helps us improve our memory.

2. Sleep helps us lengthen our lives.

3. Sleep helps our creativity.

4. Sleep helps our daily performance.

5. Sleep helps us improve our grades [if we are studying].

6. Sleep helps sharpen our attention.

7. Sleep helps us maintain a healthy weight.

8. Sleep helps reduce levels of stress.

9. Sleep helps us avoid accidents

10. Sleep helps us control our emotions.

Our lives can only travel one road at a time. Our minds, however, can travel the entire globe all at once. It's exhausting to have an overactive, anxious mind. This is all part of our self-control package. You need to control the emotional tension between your will and your mind. Do whatever you can do to not let your emotions run away.

Hey runaway. Please don't runaway.

At bedtime, our bodies may be horizontal, but our minds might be fully awake. Our bodies may be securely tucked into bed, but our minds might be running away from some fear. We need to understand the power of sleep and the fact that we have been wired and designed by God to need sleep. We need to give Him our rest. We need to give Him our sleep. This is our will in action, choosing to lay it all down. We need to sleep in His peace. We need to sleep in His grace. The good news is, when we sleep, God doesn't. When we can't sleep because of stress or worry, we should remember this truth, that God is on duty 24/7, watching over us as we sleep. Our God neither slumbers nor sleeps. We can't humanly handle a 24/7 life, so we must do this thing called sleep. We need to give our sleep to God as an offering, which is, "I choose, Lord God, to not control my 24/7 life. I need to have a little rest now and let you watch over my life, because while I'm sleeping, Father, You are not."

Have you ever told a little child, "You're just tired"? They'll likely reply, "No, I am not tired! I'm not tired! I'm not tired, Mommy." To which you might reply, "You're over-tired, child. Go to bed." Some of us actually behave like that. And no one is going to come alongside us and say, "You're just over-tired", because no one wants to deal with us and our emotions. The fact is – if you are over-tired you aren't going to be rational. You're going to be teary. And if it's that time of the month, heaven help us all! Add hormones to sleeplessness and you become an emotional train wreck waiting to happen – you need to go to bed!

Rest for the soul is provided in the presence of God. We have to keep looking after our natural bodies and our spiritual soul. Sleep is such a significant part of our human experience. It's no wonder the Bible mentions it so frequently.

The Bible makes reference to "Literal Sleep" and "Symbolic Sleep."

LITERAL SLEEP

The word "sleep" is used to describe the state of the body in normal, unconscious rest. On one occasion, when Jesus and His disciples were crossing the Sea of Galilee, the Lord was sleeping on a cushion in the boat [Mark 4:38]. The Lord is out. The Lord is GONE. The Lord is asleep. Fully at peace, fully trusting. He is having rest. This proves the true humanity of our Savior – He needed some sleep! In ministry, sometimes we think we are above and beyond that, and we think we can keep on going. I have a phrase that's tongue in cheek, which is "We can sleep in heaven." There are some projects and things that we do that require us to work long hours – and some of it is necessary and perhaps some of it will amount to nothing in heaven. We need sleep! We need to make sure we are allocating enough time to get enough proper sleep so we are functioning well in our awake time.

SYMBOLIC SLEEP

The term "sleep" is used symbolically in several different ways in the Bible. Sometimes sleep is used as the equivalent of being lazy. Sometimes sleep is used to represent spiritual lethargy. Sometimes sleep can be used to represent being unprepared. These three things scare me: laziness, spiritual lethargy, and being unprepared. I pray they scare you, too. If they don't bother you at all, you will live with them, and you will just spend your life wandering around aimlessly. Make a decision to dislike any laziness that comes into your life. Recognize spiritual lethargy and slap it sideways. Give your inner child a loud and clear wake up call. And be prepared!

#biblesays

"Come to me, all you who are weary and burdened, and I will give you rest. Take my yoke upon you and learn from me, for I am gentle and humble in heart, and you will find rest for your souls. For my yoke is easy and my burden is light."

matthew chapter eleven verses twenty-eight to thirty
new living translation

There are many stories in the Bible about Jesus coming back at the end of time. Some people are ready for His return while others are not. We need to be prepared in life, but we also need to be prepared for Jesus to come back. It is not okay to be unprepared. It is this kind of sleep that we need to be careful of. We need to wake up!

We need to sleep, and restless or sleepless nights don't help us in our body or soul. If you aren't sleeping well perhaps take a look at some practical things you could change to help you sleep in heavenly peace. Following are some practical things that we can change for the better:

7 Reasons We Can't Sleep:

1. Your bedroom may not be dark enough.

2. Your mattress and pillow may be old and uncomfortable.

3. What we eat and what we drink, especially at night, can affect our sleep.

4. Your bedroom temperature may be too warm or too cold.

5. Clockwatching.

6. Watching TV [or looking at your computer or cell phone screen].

7. Worrying about your problems.

There is a time to sleep – but it is not at harvest time. That's why I say we can sleep in Heaven – because there is work to be done for God's Kingdom now, while we are still on earth.

#biblesays

"A wise youth harvests in the summer, but one who sleeps during harvest is a disgrace."

proverbs chapter ten verse five
new living translation

Jesus said, "The laborers are few." The harvest is here. The lost are all around us, all the time. We need to pray God helps us deal with our laziness, spiritual lethargy, and being ill prepared. We need to be energetic, spiritually vibrant, and we need to be prepared and ready for service.

We do need literal, physical sleep. We're humans – we're not designed to be awake for 24 hours a day – working, worrying, wasting time. We need to sleep knowing the Almighty never slumbers nor sleeps.

7 Keys to Sleeping in Heavenly Peace:

1. Make your peace with God.

[repent, turn away from your old life]

There is no guilt or condemnation in Christ Jesus. So if you go to sleep feeling guilty – that did not come from the Lord. There is no need for you to go to sleep feeling guilty, and waking up in the night and feeling guilty, and then waking up in the morning and feeling guilty, and then walking around all day feeling guilty. If you have done something wrong before the Lord, make amends. Repent, which means you say, "I am sorry," and then never do it again. Having remorse means you're sorry, but you leave yourself open to being able to do it again. Repentance means that you actually turn away and walk in the other direction completely.

2. Make peace with people.

[go to your brother]

Make your peace with God and make your peace with people, because it is usually people who keep us awake at night. Projects can do this – but it's normally a project relating to people. It's either for people or from people. Make your peace with people. The Bible talks about that in Matthew 18. We need to go to our brother. If he doesn't listen, take a friend. And if he still doesn't listen, there is a process involved in making peace and doing it properly. If your brother hurts you and your brother wrongs you and upsets you – still sleep on it, and if you make it through the night, then let it be. Not every grievance that ever happens to you requires a "pow-wow" confrontation. If something keeps you awake at night, then you must fix it. So sleep on it and give it one night's rest. If you can't forgive and move on, you need to go to them. You can't go to someone else about the person. If you go to someone about them, you might lose them. Go straight to the person that hurt you. This usually solves it. If you can't go to them, because they refuse to talk to you or for some other reason outside of your control, there is no other option. The Bible does not give us another pattern. So, if you don't have the courage to go to them, or you don't have the conviction that it will actually be fixed, then take it to the Lord and go to sleep. There is a process for everything.

3. **Make peace with yourself.**
   [behold He makes all things new]
   We can all be unwise at times. Perhaps you, like me, sometimes go to sleep playing a conversation with yourself over and over about how you wish you had not said what you said, or how you wish you had not done something. Perhaps you missed an opportunity to say or do something positive but didn't take action, and now can't stop thinking about it. Over-thinking is a big sleep disturber. We need to make peace with ourselves.

4. **Make peace with your past.**
   [forgive us our trespasses...]
   When did that issue occur? A while ago? You don't need to take it into your future. Make peace with your past. Whether that past

pain was self-inflicted, or other inflicted. You need to make peace with it. You need to get to a point where you accept the fact that if it is irreconcilable on earth, it will be reconciled in heaven. The books balance in Heaven. Most of us are waiting for something to be reconciled on Earth, but some things will only be reconciled in Heaven.

5. Make peace with your present.

    [come to me, all who are weary and heavy burdened]

    Often, this is the most uncomfortable place for us to live: in our "now." We find ourselves unsatisfied with our present because we want our tomorrow so badly, or we want our yesterday to go away, or maybe we want it to come back. It's time to make peace with your present. I have learned to make peace with my present and to trust God with my future.

6. Make peace with your future.

    [know the plans I have for you, says the Lord…]

    This is how you and I make peace with our future. We pray: "Father, not my will – but Your will be done." We don't pray a silly prayer like "God, my will be done." [God, please deliver me from my will!] Learn to pray, "Lord, I set before you my future and everything that it holds." Make peace with your future as you leave it in God's hands.

7. Make peace through prayer.

    [don't worry about anything, but pray about everything]

    Remember, God is on the night shift, every single night. This is what the Bible says about enjoying a good night's sleep:

#biblesays

"Dear friend, guard Clear Thinking and Common Sense with your life; don't for a minute lose sight of them. They'll keep your soul alive and well, they'll keep you fit and attractive. You'll travel safely, you'll neither tire nor trip. You'll take afternoon naps without a worry, you'll enjoy a good night's sleep. No need to panic over alarms or surprises, or predictions that doomsday's just around the corner, Because God will be right there with you; he'll keep you safe and sound."

proverbs chapter three verses twenty-one to twenty-six
the message

Sadly, some people live in a permanent state of worry. They can't sleep at night on their own. Many of them are medicated so they are able to sleep at night, and simply pop a pill. That's no way to live. We need to be able to sleep naturally. We need to be able to sleep in heavenly peace.

If you are using medication to sleep, and your doctor says you need it for now, my prayer for you is that it will be short. Nothing is for eternity except eternity. We need to ask God to help us by sending the Holy Spirit to comfort us to sleep, everyday.

We need to train ourselves to be sleepers. I have not slept properly since my last baby. I don't know if I ever will again, but I am determined I'm not going to start medicating myself to sleep. I would rather be tired than make a decision to knock myself out every night because I don't know what else to do.

However, if you are unsure as to why you are unable to sleep, it may be a good idea to seek medical assistance. There could be a simple non-medicated remedy available to help you get some good sleep. We need to always remember that in our sleeping, God is very active. While Adam was sleeping, God created Eve. While "he" Adam, was sleeping, "He" God, was watching. While he was sleeping, He was working. While we are sleeping, God is with us and will always be with us.

Humanity has been created to enjoy sleep so that God can be established in our lives as The Almighty. In our sleeping, it is His wake time. Can we trust him that much? Approach tonight with a little more intention. We get into bed because we are tired. We get into bed because it is bedtime, but when was the last time you thought to yourself that your sleeping is an offering to the Lord, therefore I am going to sleep well. When I wake up and worry, I understand now that this is not what God intended. I don't mean we will stop waking up and worrying, but I'm presenting a different approach.

#biblesays

"God put the Man into a deep sleep. As he slept He removed one of his ribs and replaced it with flesh. God then used the rib that He had taken from the Man to make Woman and presented her to the Man."

genesis chapter two verses twenty-one to twenty-two
the message

A child who sleeps is a blessing to their parent. A child who doesn't protest or negotiate, or stall or struggle is a blessing to their parent. A child who is able to sleep peacefully through the night is a happy child when he or she awakens. We need to learn to sleep like a baby sleeps.

So how do we present our "sleep" to God as an offering? By not protesting, by not struggling, by not worrying and by obediently laying our heads on our pillow and allowing peace and rest to envelop our body, soul, and spirit.

A number of years ago when my Dad was diagnosed with cancer, I remember one night waking up and sensing a presence near me. The presence wasn't physical, it was something I sensed in my spirit. It was like the soft security of a warm blanket on a cold winter's night enveloping me and comforting me. I woke up my husband Jonathan and asked him if the Holy Spirit hovers over people, close to their bodies, and he assured me that He does. He assured me that the Holy Spirit is our Comforter and He provides comfort when we need it most. That night a blanket covered my body, but God knew I needed a blanket of comfort over my spirit and soul. It was the most amazing experience, and one I will never ever forget.

God healed my Dad and the doctors declared it a miracle!

He [our Father in Heaven] gives His beloved [us] sleep. Let's be committed to not allowing the sun to go down on our madness or on our sadness. Don't go to bed mad, or sad. Let's wipe the slate clean every single night so we can awake afresh every single day. Go to bed confidently knowing He is watching, working, and willfully caring for us.

Let's cast our cares on Him because He cares for us.

GOODNIGHT!

#gone

"Father, we thank thee for the night, and for the pleasant morning light; For rest and food and loving care, and all that makes the day so fair. Help us to do the things we should, to be to others kind and good; In all we do, in work or play, to grow more loving every day."[4]

Rebecca Weston
1890

4

eating

to take into the body by the mouth for digestion, energy and enjoyment

#anonymous

Jesus' hidden years … and yours

"No parade. No drum roll. Not even an explanation. Jesus allowed Himself to be thought of as a sinner… Something in surrendering to hiddenness strengthened Jesus to not make a name for Himself, to not be His own PR person. Something in embracing that prolonged season of obscurity enabled Him to appear to be less in order to be able to do more. Hidden years, when heeded, empower a soul to patiently trust God with their press releases. All that waiting actually grants us the strength to wait a little longer and not rush God's plans for our lives."[5]

Alicia Britt Chole
Anonymous

Food. Glorious food!

I love food and I love eating. My mother loves to tell stories of me as a baby and toddler and how content I was to just sit and eat and watch the world go by. When I was a teenager however, I was afraid to eat in front of people. One year, as a teen, I was away at a youth summer camp for two weeks and barely ate anything at all. In fact, the situation was so bad the leader in charge of the camp took me aside and told me that everyone was calling me "Anna" [short for anorexic], and said if I didn't eat I would have to go home. He said, "If you don't eat, you won't poop and if you don't poop, you'll die." At that moment, I didn't care about what would happen to me, I was just so embarrassed that people had noticed and were talking about me. The very thing I feared most was attention from people, and yet by skipping meals and thinking no one noticed, people were now watching me closer than ever. I was caught in a sad cycle of dysfunction.

Now, I'm grateful to be able to say I can eat in front of people. I am completely over that awkward phase of my life and I have moved into a phase of "the foodie," the exact opposite! So now I have to be careful not to overindulge – whether in private or in public.

I love food so much I usually say grace before all three courses, and especially before I eat dessert. However, grace isn't only a prayer to say at mealtime, grace is a way to live. I've learned to live in the grace of God when it comes to being able to enjoy food and yet not allow it to rule my life. One of my favorite movies growing up was "Willy Wonka And The Chocolate Factory" with Gene Wilder released in 1971. One of my favorite characters, apart from Charlie and his Grandpa, was Veruca Salt. If you remember that movie, then please remember to never be like her. Her behavior in the movie is very funny, but the overwhelming obsession with food in America is not funny. Food is important, but food should not be our obsession.

The Bible has much to say about eating and drinking.

#biblesays

"For the Kingdom of God is not a matter of eating and drinking, but of righteousness, peace and joy in the Holy Spirit."
romans chapter fourteen verse seventeen
new international version

"Therefore I tell you, do not worry about your life, what you will eat or drink; or about your body, what you will wear. Is not life more important than food, and the body more important than clothes?"
matthew chapter six verse twenty-five
new international version

"Eating too much honey [sugar] can make you sick."
proverbs twenty-five verse sixteen
new living translation

Let's jump on board the grace train for a moment. I want to let you know I am living this journey right now and still working it out. Let's give ourselves and each other grace in the area of eating and food, because this subject can be more complicated than what meets the eye. Look at little Veruca. You might think, "Oh, she's just a little tiny thing. Surely she can have 16 donuts." We often judge someone who might not be our size, thinking, "Oh, they must overeat." To be honest, we don't know anything. This subject is not about whether you are overweight or not. It is about whether you eat too much, because we only need to eat the amount we need to nourish our bodies.

God gave us food to enjoy. God didn't give us food so we would become obsessed about it. We need to learn to feed our bodies instead of using food to feed our emotions. We need to eat because it's mealtime, whatever time that is, and not because we are happy, sad, bored, stressed, or just because the food is sitting there, just because we can, just because somebody brought it into work, or just because it's left over. Eat when you need to – don't eat for all those other reasons.

Food is for fuel. Food isn't to fuel our feelings. Fuel food gives you enjoyment by way of energy and longevity. This is not about dieting, it's about having boundaries around what you eat. Make the food you eat the most fun food of your life. Don't think that your healthy fuel food has to be boring! Make the food you eat the food you love. If you don't love it, find something you love! There is very little restriction – it's all in our head.

There are so many wonderful fuel foods we can eat that will not only make us feel good, but that also taste great! We need to change our mindset that might tell us healthy eating is boring and flavorless. That is so far from the truth! Remember, fast food gives you instant elation, followed by instant deflation.

#biblesays

"God said to Moses, 'I'm going to rain bread down from the skies for you. The people will go out and gather each day's ration. I'm going to test them to see if they'll live according to my Teaching or not. On the sixth day, when they prepare what they have gathered, it will turn out to be twice as much as their daily ration.'"

exodus chapter sixteen verses four and five

the message

"The people of Israel went to work and started gathering, some more, some less, but when they measured out what they had gathered, those who gathered more had no extra and those who gathered less weren't short – each person had gathered as much as was needed."

exodus chapter sixteen verses seventeen and eighteen

the message

From the beginning of time, God has had a plan for us when it comes to food and eating. If we get into His Word, we see there is so much truth that can help us to set up these healthy boundaries for our lives. The Bible in Exodus 16 talks about how God delivered the Israelites from Egypt and Moses was their leader.

The Israelites complained about not having enough food to eat. They were used to eating all kinds of food in Egypt, but they had forgotten they were also forced to make bricks without straw. God delivered them from a life of slavery and the first thing they complained about was their grumbling stomachs. "We're hungry now. You brought us out here to starve to death." God heard their grumbling. God sent them food, and He sent them instructions about the food. God ensured they would continue to rely on Him.

Have you ever sat down at a table with someone and wondered how they could have eaten as much as they did? Where does all that food go? Every one of us has been designed and created by God differently, uniquely. And that includes our metabolism. Be set free! Some of us only need a little, so when we eat a little, it's all we need. Other people need more, so if you need to eat more, that's fine too. However, if you eat more than you need, you're going to have excess to deal with. Each one of us needs to determine our boundaries. I love that the Bible says, "Those who needed a little didn't have anything left over. Those who needed a lot didn't have anything left over." This means we can leave people who need more food than us alone. We don't need to criticize people who have a different metabolism than us.

Pray and thank God for His Word, and for truth that we are searching for. Thank God that we are going to find answers and solutions in this area of our lives. We need revelation. GONE is a revelation. Let's thank God that He has designed each of us beautifully, uniquely, and differently. As we discover who we are in Him, and how we're wired, let's allow the Holy Spirit to help us discover what food we need for optimum energy and enjoyment, everyday. Let's ask God to help us find true freedom in this area of our lives.

I was at lunch with great friends Stovall and Kerri Weems in Jacksonville Florida, and we had just eaten lunch, and it was a lovely meal. I always appreciate being at a place where I can order grilled lean meat and steamed vegetables. That's a treat for me because it's what I eat, and within my boundary. I find this kind of food delicious, and don't get bored with it. I particularly enjoy the fact that I don't feel sick afterwards because the food hasn't been fried. We finished the meal. I could see the waiter passing around a tray of desserts set inside shot glasses. I actually saw him as soon as I walked in. I was following him, thinking, "Oh my goodness, those desserts look so amazing. And they're so little!" At the end of our meal, he brought the desserts over to our table, put them right in front of us, and proceeded to tell us about these tiny, little desserts, most of them only half filling the glass. I thought, "Let's get all of them and I'll have a bite of each one." The server proceeded to tell us how many calories were in each shot glass. Ah! I almost wished he hadn't told me! "Well, thank you, kind sir, for that information," I said, "Information is all powerful, and I can't indulge, since now I know what's in them." I asked the kind sir to bring me the check without the dessert. Every single one of those desserts was between 190-250 calories and only the size of a half shot glass! Most of us would not balk at that. We wouldn't even think about it because it's the equivalent of two teaspoons of someone else's dessert. The problem is, we do need to start thinking about it. We can't just be disciplined, we need more than discipline - we also need integrity. What is integrity? Knowing right and doing right. When you know right and do wrong, you feel guilty - you don't want that guilt. Could I have had just one dessert? Yes, but not if I had one yesterday, and the day before.

#biblesays

"The woman was convinced. She saw that the tree was beautiful and its fruit looked delicious, and she wanted the wisdom it would give her. So she took some of the fruit and ate it. Then she gave some to her husband, who was with her, and he ate it, too."

genesis chapter three verse six
new living translation

Yes, I can do anything, but not everything is beneficial. Yes, I can eat anything, but not everything is beneficial. This is important to know: if you eat just 200 calories a day more than you need and you do that over the course of a year, you'll put on a solid 10 pounds of body fat. Not water weight, but body fat, which is much harder to lose. If you were to do that for two years, you'd put on 20 pounds. If you were to do that for five years, you would put on 50 pounds and five sizes! You were 45 years old, now you're 50, and you wonder what on earth happened? It was one of those little shot glasses of something every day. When I did the math about those 200 calories and found that out, it changed my life. Knowledge is power.

When I was pregnant with London at the age of 39, I gained 75 pounds. I honestly didn't know if I would be able to lose the weight. I figured that it would be much harder for me as a 40 year old than it was for me as a 30 year old, when I was pregnant with my daughter Bella ten years earlier. I embarked on my weight loss journey when London was around 18 months old. It took me seven months of diligent eating and exercise and I not only managed to lose the weight but also ended up in better shape than I was before the pregnancy.

The good news is, if you maintain healthy eating and exercise, you can maintain a healthy body shape. I have had to be diligent every year to ensure that I stay within range of my target weight. It is normal to gain a little weight every year, especially around Thanksgiving and Christmas, but dealing with it in the New Year is imperative.

Having experienced weight gain and then weight loss, I know how important it is to stay on top and to make sure I don't allow those little 200 extra calories a day, everyday, to creep into my eating. One of the biggest causes of lack of action in the area of healthy eating and exercise is guilt. Guilt keeps us feeling bad and stops our freedom. We need to stay on the personal "grace train." Don't be hard on yourself. Try your best everyday and if you fail, then try again tomorrow. Eventually you will tire of letting yourself down. We have all been at that point in our lives and there does come a time when we need to address poor habits, and poor mindsets. We need a food budget just like a money budget; we need to consider and account for all incoming and all outgoing foods.

Our problem with food started in the Garden of Eden. God said, don't eat fruit from a certain tree. Eve decided she knew better. God wanted his creation to trust him. Eve wanted to eat. Food is one of God's best ideas! Adam and Eve had access to every type of food in the Garden of Eden. He simply asked that they stay away from one tree. This, I believe, is our problem. When it comes to food, we need to know what to eat and what not to eat. Eve did not master food. Food mastered her. God gave mankind boundaries for a reason.

The fall of man happened over food. The fall of man happened over eating. We need healthy boundaries. Imagine going to the market and being able to have absolutely anything in the entire store, except for one thing. God said, "Don't have that one thing." We live in a poverty mentality when we think that eating well is a restriction in our life. That boundary is the most freeing thing you can find. Adam and Eve had access to every type of food but were asked not eat that one type. This is our challenge: when it comes to food, we simply need to know what to eat and what not to eat.

When it comes to food, there are many different people with diverse different philosophies, but I like what the Bible says, which is that you can eat anything. I prefer God's Word on the subject. Different people have certain habits and may take part in different customs for religious or cultural reasons. They won't eat certain things because of their particular religious or cultural reasons. Since Jesus said it is all good to eat, we should choose according to our conscience. What God has declared okay for us to eat is okay for us to eat. Let's not become guilty when it comes to eating food God has declared okay. Let's approach this whole garden of food with absolute freedom.

#biblesays

"The next day as the three travelers were approaching the town, Peter went out on the balcony to pray. It was about noon. Peter got hungry and started thinking about lunch. While lunch was being prepared, he fell into a trance. He saw the skies open up. Something that looked like a huge blanket lowered by ropes at its four corners settled on the ground. Every kind of animal and reptile and bird you could think of was on it. Then a voice came: 'Go to it, Peter—kill and eat.' Peter said, 'Oh, no, Lord. I've never so much as tasted food that was not kosher.' The voice came a second time: 'If God says it's okay, it's okay.' This happened three times, and then the blanket was pulled back up into the skies."

acts chapter ten verses nine to sixteen
the message

Approach the garden of food with freedom, and then make your selections on what you need. What do you need? Sometimes I need a little bit of chocolate, so I'll have a little bit of chocolate, but will make sure it falls within my boundary. We need boundaries and balance when it comes to healthy eating. The Bible says all food is good but not all food is beneficial, especially if we eat it all at once!

Jesus was a foodie, I'm sure. He ate with sinners, He ate with tax collectors, and He ate with His disciples. He used food to build friendships and to further His ministry and build the Kingdom. Food is a fantastic thing, and we should enjoy it! We must also know and use our boundaries. In Matthew 11:19, Jesus was accused of being a glutton and a drunkard by religious leaders. Jesus enjoyed food, but he certainly did not overindulge. Something wonderful happens when you eat with freedom. People might think you're indulging but you are just eating free.

I enjoy food. I love what it does for me, I love how I feel, I love the flavor, I love everything about it. Some may think I'm being a glutton because I'm enjoying myself, but believe me I have much needed boundaries for myself. Those boundaries have changed my life forever.

What happens when we consistently overindulge in food? Gluttony! Gluttony is an inordinate desire to consume more than one requires. The word "gluttony" is derived from the Latin "gluttire," which means "to gulp down or swallow." This means overindulgence and overconsumption of food, drink, or wealth items, to the point of extravagance or waste. Gluttony is habitual eating to excess.

Gluttony is different from the 200 calorie daily excess I mentioned earlier. If you have found yourself to be five sizes bigger than you used to be, please hop aboard the grace train and stay on the grace train, because you can't deal with a challenging eating issue with guilt. Where there is grace, there's no guilt. It may not have been gluttonous behavior that got you there.

#biblesays

"You say, 'I am allowed to do anything' but not everything is good for you. You say, 'I am allowed to do anything' but not everything is beneficial."

one corinthians chapter ten verse twenty-three
new living translation

#gone

"Gluttony denotes, not any desire of eating and drinking, but an inordinate desire... leaving the order of reason, wherein the good of moral virtue consists."[1]

Thomas Aquinas – Medieval Theologian

It may be that you didn't know that just a little spoonful here and a little spoonful there could make such a profound impact. Perhaps you didn't realize that as we get older we cannot afford to eat as many calories as we used to because our metabolism slows down with age. I want all the skinny people reading this who love a big buffet to stop thinking that people who are overweight must be gluttons. We have no idea how or why they arrived at this place. Most of the time, weight creeps on incrementally, and not because we sit down to eat 16 donuts for breakfast every morning.

Gluttony is not a matter of, "Oh, I would love to eat that. That would be really nice." It's an inordinate desire where we cannot control ourselves anymore. We might think that we can overindulge in secret, but we can't do anything in secret before God, or even before ourselves.

Thomas Aquinas took a more expansive view of gluttony, arguing that it could also include an obsessive anticipation of meals, and the constant eating of delicacies and excessively costly foods. Thomas Aquinas writes about six ways to commit gluttony:[2]

- Praepropere
  Eating too soon. Eating, and eating, and eating and we don't wait until it's our mealtime.

- Laute
  Eating too expensively. Ordering food we can't afford.

- Nimis
  Eating too much.

- Ardenter
  Eating too eagerly.

- **Studiose**
  Eating too daintily or elaborately.

- **Forente**
  Eating wildly or out of control.

Gluttony is not solely an overweight person's problem. This is everyone's problem, if we are not careful. Do not allow your appetite to be your god. Don't allow your desire for food to distract you or cause you to lose focus on what is really important. Look at Esau in Genesis Chapter 25; he traded his birthright in for a bowl of stew. "I need to have it now. My rumbling tummy!" Gluttony is all about the focus of our stomach. That is a problem of the overeater. That is a problem of the under eater. That is a problem of the staunch, perfect eater. Any kind of obsession when it comes to food is going to hurt us. Whether it is being so careful with food that you can't go out anywhere and enjoy eating with others, or whether you feel as though you are starving all the time because you are actually under-caloried – we need balance. Yes, we need boundaries, and yes we need balance. We need to set boundaries, but we also need to know when we have gone too far in our focus on our stomachs.

I was on a ministry trip and, unfortunately, I didn't eat for 24 hours. Once upon a time, just before a school dance, not eating for a day or two would mean fitting into a pair of skintight jeans, but that isn't my motivation anymore. On that trip, I simply couldn't find any type of food that was suitable in order for me to be healthy in body and soul. The options were terrible, and I kept thinking and expecting at any moment I'd find something I could eat that wouldn't make me sick, or put me in a "food coma" so I couldn't think.

I have boundaries and sometimes that makes life on the road difficult. However, without these healthy boundaries I'd be in poor health and have little energy to do what's required of me.

#biblesays

"Dear brothers and sisters, pattern your lives after mine, and learn from those who follow our example. For I have told you often before, and I say it again with tears in my eyes, that there are many whose conduct shows they are really enemies of the cross of Christ. They are headed for destruction. Their god is their appetite, they brag about shameful things, and they think only about this life here on earth."

philippians chapter three verses seventeen to nineteen
new living translation

Our minds need to be engaged in other things apart from just our stomachs. That's why I don't weigh myself every day. If you are on a weight-loss program, you need to weigh as often as your program says you should weigh. But if you are in maintenance mode, weighing yourself every single day could actually be detrimental to your mental and emotional health!

With water fluctuations, hormones, or whatever else, I can't afford to have a bad day in my head. I put on my clothes and immediately I know, "Oh, I need to fix that." Still, I need a certain freedom in my life, and I'm still living and working this out. I don't have time for a "bad day." That's why I stay within my own personal boundaries that include incidental moments when I am at the mercy of others.

Following is some interesting information about food and eating in the USA:[3-9]

- The average American spends $151 a week on food. That is $7,852.00 a year.
- There are currently 308.6 million Americans.
- That is a yearly figure of over 2 trillion dollars Americans spend on food.
- 40 percent of food in the U.S. goes to waste.
- The current annual revenue of the U.S. weight loss industry, including diet books, diet drugs and weight loss surgeries is $20 billion dollars.
- There are approximately 108 million people on diets in the United States.
- Dieters typically make four to five attempts per year.
- 85% of customers consuming weight-loss products and services are female.
- Americans spend an additional $15 billion each year on cosmetic surgery.
- The number of liposuction procedures has increased by 111%.

"Gluttony is not a secret vice."[10]

Orson Welles

- "Tummy tucks" are up by 147%.
- By 2030, roughly 42 percent of Americans will be morbidly obese.
- This staggering projection comes with a $550 billion major healthcare price tag.
- The average overweight [non-active] woman [180 pounds] burns about 2,000 calories a day.
- Just one pound of body fat represents an excess of 3,500 calories in the average body.
- To lose one pound of body fat every week, you have to burn 500 calories more than you eat, every day.
- To lose two pounds of body fat every week, you have to burn 1,000 calories more than you eat, every day.

MEN

- On average, an active 25-year-old man needs 2,800 calories with 30-60 minutes of moderate activity every day.
- On average, an active 50-year-old man needs 2,600 calories with 30 to 60 minutes of moderate activity every day.

WOMEN

- On average, an active 25-year-old woman needs 2,200 calories with 30-60 minutes of moderate activity every day.
- On average, a sedentary 60-year-old woman needs 1,600 calories.

Let's make the most of our freedom now while it matters!

Remember, if we eat just 200 calories per day more than we need, we will gain 10 pounds in one year. If we do that for 5 years in a row, we will gain 50 pounds, and 5 sizes!

#biblesays

"The boundary lines have fallen for me in pleasant places;
surely I have a delightful inheritance."

psalm chapter sixteen verse six
new international version

#gone

Is everything permissible? YES!
Is everything profitable? NO!

- Plain bagel without cream cheese – 280 calories
  [to burn is 32 minutes of jogging].
  It also is not building muscle and is building fat.

- 1 medium coffee with cream & sugar - 180 calories
  [to burn is 50 minutes of walking]

- Half a cup of trail mix - 190 calories
  [to burn is 29 minutes of cycling]

- Strawberry & banana smoothie - 370 calories
  [to burn is 103 minutes of walking]

- Yogurt parfait with honey & granola - 300 calories
  [to burn is 34 minutes of jogging]

- Small bowl of vegetable soup - 160 calories
  [to burn is 24 minutes of cycling]

- 1 cup of raisin bran cereal - no milk – 190 calories
  [to burn is 53 minutes of walking][11]

Is everything permissible? Yes! Is everything profitable? No! Choose wisely! We need to look at what we're feeding our bodies as fuel. We only need to eat what we need. If we eat what we need, we won't have to deal with the consequences of overeating.

I don't know why "working out" isn't called "working off." It's like debt. We know we have to get rid of it. We need to know what "fuel" is and what "entertainment" is. Our favorite sugary latte from our favorite coffee house isn't a food group. It's entertainment [that should save us calories and dollars right there]. We need food budget boundaries! Psalm 16:6 in the Bible says, "The boundary lines have fallen for me in pleasant places; surely I have a delightful inheritance."

I can truly say, "My boundary lines have fallen for me in pleasant places." I have a delightful inheritance when I stay within my personal boundaries. We need to maximize calories. If I only have so many calories, I am going to make sure they are yummy. Food I eat must taste good, be good for me, and can't give me a tummy ache later. It can't pick me up one second and drop me down to the ground the next. I don't have time for that. I need something that is going to be fueling my body all day long.

We also need to maximize our exercise. If you don't have a heart rate monitor, you won't know how much fat you're burning. You might as well sit down and have a really intense conversation over coffee, since you would probably burn as much fat as you would going for a stroll. If you are going to go for a stroll you like to smell roses – do that, but make sure you do your cardio first. Always maximize your opportunities.

5 STEPS FORWARD:

1. Create a food budget.
   - How much fuel do you need each day?
   - How much exercise do you need each day?

Create a food budget, just like you would a time budget or a financial budget. Find out how much fuel you need per day. Because whatever you need – you should enjoy it. Enjoy your fuel. Find out how much exercise you need as well, because then you can eat more fuel.

2. Pace yourself.
   - Spread your fuel out over the day.
   - Enjoy 5 small meals every day.

Pace yourself! Spread your fuel out over the day. Don't ever be caught without something you need. Try to eat 5-6 small meals instead of 3 large ones.

3. Wait 20 minutes for the fuel to register in your "tummy tank."
   - Let the food hit the "account."
   - Drink water but don't eat more fuel.

Right after breakfast, I'm starving for lunch. I feel like I could eat my whole breakfast and entire lunch [and probably yours too!]. Am I actually starving and do I actually need all that food at breakfast time? No – the food just has not hit the tank yet. I've learned I need to wait 20 minutes. If I go ahead and eat more, it's not going to help me. I need to walk away. I have 20 minutes where I know that the fuel is still hitting the tank. Once it hits the tank you will be satisfied. Give yourself a few minutes for the fuel to register. Drink water if you can't cope, but don't eat more fuel.

4. Increase expenditure [exercise].
   - Sow energy.
   - Reap energy.

Increase your expenditure. If you sow energy, you'll reap energy! Make sure you're doing some form of exercise, and make do it as regularly as you possibly can. We don't reap energy from sleep. We reap rest from sleep. We reap energy when we sow energy.

5. **Feed your body, not your emotions.**
   - Eat what you need.
   - And love what you need - be creative with food within your boundaries

   Feed your body, not your emotions. If you find yourself going to the refrigerator frequently outside of mealtimes, put something on the refrigerator door to remind you of your goals and boundaries. It might be a picture that inspires you or some goals that you've written down. Eat what you need and love to eat what you need. God has given us freedom. He has given us food and we should enjoy the food. Don't put yourself on a severe, restrictive diet. If we don't stop feeding our feelings, we are going to live with ridiculous amounts of guilt. World-renowned psychologist Dr. Robi Sonderegger says that guilt is the precursor to repeat behavior. Instead, we need to get on the grace train. If we don't come at this issue from a position of grace, we are going to set ourselves up to fail. We need to give ourselves grace and also give grace to other people. Let other people work themselves out. Whatever you do... find your freedom, and find your boundaries.

When I look at all the celebration that takes place over the course of a calendar year, it is no wonder so many people have a problem with food.

We celebrate so many holidays around food. We need to not allow a holiday or celebration to sneak up on us. We need to be savvy and smarter than that. Look at this list of all the occasions we have to celebrate during the year!

#gone

BODY+SOUL+SPIRIT

"If the enemy knows you live by your feelings, he will feed you everything you feel like."

Dianne Wilson

IT'S PARTY TIME!

- New Year
- Super Bowl
- Valentine's Day
- Easter
- Mother's Day
- Memorial Day
- Graduation Day
- Father's Day
- Fourth of July
- Summer
- Labor Day
- Harvest [pumpkin, costume and candy party time]
- Thanksgiving
- Christmas

And that's not all! There are birthdays, weddings, anniversaries and the list goes on, and on, and on.

Whatever time of year it is right now, "Happy New Year to you!" Our New Year's resolutions are in full effect at the start of the year, but then 6 weeks later comes Valentine's Day! If you start eating well in the New Year, by February 14th you will have your first test. What are you going to do? Are you going to cave in? Just a few weeks later, there's Easter, so you might as well roll Valentine's Day into Easter. Chocolate, chocolate, chocolate – all the time. This is how it happens! Followed by Mothers Day! "Oh, I work so hard, and I give my everything all the time. Can't I just sit down, be waited on, and eat all the chocolate I want?" Mother's Day is followed by Father's Day. "Well, we want to celebrate all the men in our world!"

Fourth of July comes around pretty quickly after that, and we say, "Come on! I'm celebrating summer now! This is my barbecue, this is my burger, this is my chocolate shake." Then summer comes, and I just want to have a nice time, and definitely not be anywhere near a swimming pool or bathing suit or anything like that. So maybe I'll go inside where it's air-conditioned, and eat. Then, pretty soon it's Labor Day, the last holiday before the kids go back to school. At this time of year we might say, "I'm so stressed, I'm just going to eat!" Then we have Harvest time, which is all about candy and chocolate. Again! A few weeks after that, we have Thanksgiving. Then a few weeks later, there's Christmas! Then I must enjoy myself over the holidays because they all roll together.

So I go from Christmas to New Year, and I say loud and clear, "I have to stop!" That's what you call the year that was. I haven't even mentioned the birthdays, weddings, anniversaries, school picnics or church events!

When I made that list, I thought, "Aha!" I've watched myself do this over the years, and it's really hard. You get some momentum and then you get to a holiday and your momentum takes a hit. A holiday is one day – not the whole month. Now, do we get to enjoy that day? Yes! If you have your boundaries in place, you can enjoy everything. We just have to make sure that one thing does not roll into another.

Let's give God our eating, everyday, and let us always remember that the Holy Spirit is very present to help us.

#pray

Father, Thank You for Your Word. Thank You for boundaries. Thank You that You have given them to me for my benefit, not as a rule, but as a benefit, so I can have freedom from within. Thank You that You have given me so much wonderful food and drink to enjoy. Lord, help me approach the supermarket differently, and restaurant menus differently. Help me see how much freedom there is and how much you have given me to enjoy. Lord, help me not struggle in this area and set me free please Father. I just want freedom in You. Give me grace that only You can give. Thank You for being with me and working on my behalf and helping me make this into a reality of how I am going to live the rest of my life. Thank you God for the Holy Spirit and that He is very present to help me everyday.

Amen.

5

going to work

being engaged in physical or mental activity in order to achieve a purpose
or result, especially in one's job or place of employment

#anonymous

Jesus' hidden years … and yours

"Concentrating our attention on the tasty treat dangled before us is most unwise when we are tempted in the layer of appetite. This is the fatal mistake Eve made. She did not throw out an anchor to stabilize herself. Instead, Eve tried to navigate the temptation with her desires and passions at the helm. When we commit this error in judgment, we fall prey to the 'lie of just one.' We disconnect the moment of temptation from all other moments and dismiss our inner hesitations as overreactions because, we rationalize, this is only about 'one' moment of splurging…"[12]

Alicia Britt Chole
Anonymous

Hi-ho, hi-ho, it's off to work we go!

We're going to work and we are excited about it. I love to work. I have always loved to work. I've always had a solid work ethic because of how I was raised. I have come from hard-working parents, who themselves have come from hard-working parents. I love enjoying the fruit of hard work. I don't like busy work. I don't like doing things for no reason. I have a goal. I have things I want to achieve. I like to be efficient with my time. I could not wait to get my first job, and I've worked all kinds of jobs since I was a teenager.

I was 14 years old when I started my first job. I worked at a BP gas station. It was on Liverpool Road, right next to the bowling alley. I remember answering an ad in the classifieds – back when there were no personal computers. I circled the ad. I wanted to work and I didn't care what I did. It wasn't about the money. I was excited to work! Back in those days, the hiring process was much simpler than it is today. You would call the employer on the phone and they would ask you a few questions. If they liked your responses, you got the job, and you turned up for work. There wasn't any paperwork – you just turned up for work. Simple as that! I still remember what I had for lunch that day. My Dad made me a ham and cheese sandwich to take along.

When I arrived at work that first day, I was excited because the job involved using a cash register, but that wasn't all - it also involved pressing a button to allow people to pump the gas. As the cars drove up, I'd press the button and the gas would flow. I was so excited about this, and really wanted to do well at my job. I needed more training before I could begin, though. My boss was an older man, older than my Dad. So at my first day on the job, my boss was sitting on a high chair, like a stool. And he said, "Here, I want to show you how to do something." Next thing I knew – he had pulled me towards his lap! I jumped away from him immediately, totally shocked at what a horrible dirty old man he was! Needless to say, that first day on the job at the gas station was also my last day of work at the gas station.

He sent me to get lunch for his son and I never came back. I went home instead. My parents didn't ask me why I didn't go back to work there anymore, and I didn't tell.

My next job was working at Franklin's supermarket as a "checkout chick." I loved the job because it involved a cash register, again, buttons, and people! I was really excited, except I didn't like getting called in at 6.00am to stock shelves, which was part of my job. I also didn't like having to sit in a back office counting all the money beforehand. Then after each shift I had to reconcile the money, and I was not allowed to leave until it balanced it within 10 cents. This was back in the days when there were no conveyor belts at a register, nor was there a scanner. Everything had to be done manually, by me, the checkout chick! Can you believe there was such an era? Then, I had to work out how much change to give people. This was such a long time ago there weren't even credit cards – we only accepted cash. I once gave a man $100 in change, more than he gave me in the first place. He kindly returned with the extra money. I didn't last there very long either.

I moved on, and became a cocktail waitress. Don't be shocked! I was good. I used to make $40 a night in pay and $100 a night in tips. It was because I didn't drink and I didn't fraternize. I just served really well, and so naturally I made really good tips.

After that, I became a receptionist. It was a 9 to 5 job, but I would leave work at 4.55pm. In my mind at the time, that was close enough. The next day when I arrived at work, my boss called me into his office and asked why I had stuffed all my work under my desk, and why I hadn't finished. I went home and say to my parents, "I'm quitting that job because my boss wants me to work and I have to finish my work." My parents said, "Get back to work." Later on I appreciated that something in my character was addressed. My approach to work needed to change.

Then I became a travel agent, but I refused to travel anywhere! My boss would say, "I'm sending you on a trip," and it would be something like a first class trip to New Zealand or some other amazing adventure, and I would say, "No, thanks!" One day my boss told me, "I'm sending you for counseling because there is something seriously wrong with you. I'm trying to send you on an amazing trip and you're saying no. What is wrong with you?" I didn't want to go anywhere because I loved home so much. Can you see how upside down my thinking was, and how afraid I was of everything? I'm telling you a little of my story so you'll see there's hope for everyone.

After all my training in travel and secretarial work, I became the Senior Master's secretary at a private boys' grammar school. I was only 19 at the time, and I had to have blinds installed on the windows in my office because those boys scared me! I was only a year or a year and a half older than most of the boys, and I would have to wait until they were all in class before I could go to the restroom, or out to lunch, because I was petrified. I asked myself, "Why do I have this job?" It wasn't so bad because I loved my boss and it was a good paying job. Back then we had corporal punishment in our schools, which meant that boys would often be sent to the Senior Master's office by their teachers as punishment for misbehavior.

The Senior Master would exact punishment on these boys by striking them on their backside with a cane. My office was attached to the Senior Master's office, and I could barely focus on my work knowing what was happening next door. The Senior Master would say, "Excuse me, Miss Saunders [my maiden name]. Could you give us a moment, please?" I would walk outside and almost cry. Then when it was over, I'd come back inside, whisper, "I am so sorry," and get on with my work.

I was approached by a modeling agent in my late teens, who signed me up and I worked as a model for the next few years. Not long after, I wrote a book which quickly became a national best-seller.

#gone

"What you do in your house is worth as much as if you did it up in Heaven for our Lord God. We should accustom ourselves to think of our position and work as sacred and well-pleasing to God, not on account of the position and work, but on account of the word and faith from which the obedience and the work flow."[1]

Martin Luther

Now I was an author with HarperCollins Australia Publishers and Random House Australia Publishers, with ongoing contracts for further books. I then became a TV host and magazine columnist. Soon after, I became a "sponsored personality." That entailed companies putting my image on their products and sending me checks every month to do so! This was residual income that my family and I were very grateful for at the time.

I put myself through Bible College during that same season because I wanted my mind to catch up with my heart. I wanted to understand the Bible more, so I devoted a year to full-time learning. Then I became a pastor. This wasn't what I had ever thought I would do, but it makes so much sense to me now. I love God and I love people. I love church and I love ministry.

So, from my BP gas station experience through roles that may seem random – God used all of it. I learned to serve and I learned to sow, in every single season of my work life. Where are you are right now in your working life? Are you living the dream or are you in between? Are you doing something at the moment that feels like it's a filler job, but you know there is something greater that you want to do? Wherever you are right now, if you trust God with the season you're in, He will take you exactly where he wants to take you.

The truth is: all of my best opportunities presented themselves as small, insignificant, ordinary, everyday, hard work. This is good for us to know. If opportunities present themselves as the wide end of the wedge or flashing neon lights, beware!

Are we waiting for the dream opportunity to fall into our lap without having to do the hard work? Our culture is obsessed with short cuts, miracle diets, get rich quick schemes, and you can have them all for just 30 easy payments of $19.95. Many people buy into these promises and end up disappointed and disillusioned with their lives. The problem with these "have it all now" scenarios is those that actually get all they want right away don't have the wisdom to steward it properly or the learned ability to sustain success.

Jesus came to establish the most significant work of all time, and He didn't do it with neon signs or in a short-term frenzy of followers.

Jesus worked to establish the Kingdom of God through His everyday ordinary life. He was building something of unprecedented value. He didn't cut corners or give the disciples 5 easy ways to be successful followers. He was faithful, he was thorough, He was patient, and He is the most successful man who has ever walked this earth. He is our example, even in our going to work. There are no shortcuts to success in life, and it looks like this: small, insignificant, ordinary, everyday, hard work.

Every time I worked hard and produced well, I was given more difficult work to accomplish. The reward for hard work is more hard work! If we walk away from our small opportunities they will be taken away from us and given to someone else.

We need to thank God for giving us revelation about our going-to-work life. When we understand the significance of our everyday, ordinary, sleeping, eating, going-to-work lives, we are able to maximize our lives. When we understand the importance of positive repetitive routine, it changes everything. When we are faithful with little, we will be granted much. Our ultimate goal is to be found faithful, good stewards of our time, our talent and our treasure, so we won't waste a moment that could be a moment of greatness.

Having been raised in a family with hard working parents and grandparents, it has always come naturally for me to want to work and to enjoy the sense of fulfillment at the end of a fruitful day. I was also raised to understand the principle of sowing and reaping as a part of my personal integrity. It was not from a Christian perspective as my parents didn't have a personal relationship with Jesus until I was fourteen. My parents exemplified not only an amazing work ethic, but they also exemplified how important it is to be patient when you are committed to building your life.

#biblesays

"Again, the Kingdom of Heaven can be illustrated by the story of a man going on a long trip. He called together his servants and entrusted his money to them while he was gone. He gave five bags of silver to one, two bags of silver to another, and one bag of silver to the last— dividing it in proportion to their abilities. He then left on his trip.

The servant who received the five bags of silver began to invest the money and earned five more. The servant with two bags of silver also went to work and earned two more. But the servant who received the one bag of silver dug a hole in the ground and hid the master's money.

After a long time their master returned from his trip and called them to give an account of how they had used his money. The servant to whom he had entrusted the five bags of silver came forward with five more and said, 'Master, you gave me five bags of silver to invest, and I have earned five more.' "The master was full of praise. 'Well done, my good and faithful servant. You have been faithful in handling this small amount, so now I will give you many more responsibilities. Let's celebrate together!'

The servant who had received the two bags of silver came forward and said, 'Master, you gave me two bags of silver to invest, and I have earned two more.' "The master said, 'Well done, my good and faithful servant. You have been faithful in handling this small amount, so now I will give you many more responsibilities. Let's celebrate together!'

Then the servant with the one bag of silver came and said, 'Master, I knew you were a harsh man, harvesting crops you didn't plant and gathering crops you didn't cultivate. I was afraid I would lose your money, so I hid it in the earth. Look, here is your money back.' But the master replied, 'You wicked and lazy servant! If you knew I harvested crops I didn't plant and gathered crops I didn't cultivate, why didn't you deposit my money in the bank? At least I could have gotten some interest on it.'

Then he ordered, 'Take the money from this servant, and give it to the one with the ten bags of silver. To those who use well what they are given, even more will be given, and they will have an abundance. But from those who do nothing, even what little they have will be taken away. Now throw this useless servant into outer darkness, where there will be weeping and gnashing of teeth.'"

matthew chapter twenty-five verses fourteen to thirty
new living translation

My parents taught me to never cut corners or perform hasty short-cuts to get ahead. They embraced the process of time. They taught me to sow, sow, sow and in time, I would reap, reap, reap.

I was driving not far from my house one morning and a very cool looking van caught my eye. It had shiny red paint on the panels, with shiny gold lettering – it seemed to belong to a very expensive company. The beautiful gold script lettering said, "The Company Name [I won't say what it is] and Sons" and went on to say "Curators of Fine Homes." As I pulled up alongside the red van, expecting to see a smartly dressed driver, I was honestly surprised to see an image in the driver's seat that was in direct contrast to the image presented by the exterior of that fancy red van. The driver had his leg up, his window down, his elbow on his knee with a cigarette between his fingers, and on top of all that he was swerving all over the road! I was sure that the "Company and Sons" would not be impressed at the swerving driving and the casual dude with the "whatever" attitude.

Following are some facts found in an interesting article from the Sustainable Business Forum on "Disturbing Survey on Business Ethics," by Norman Marks, April 2012:[2]

- 45% of employees have witnessed misconduct.
- 65% say they have reported the misconduct they saw.
- 22% of those who reported misconduct suffered as a direct result. This is higher than the 15% in 2009 and 12% in 2007, and should be a cause of great concern.
- The number of companies with 'weak ethics cultures" rose from 35% in 2009 to 42%.
- 34% of employees said their managers do not display ethical behavior [24% in 2009].
- That will cascade in effect through the organization, with the result that all employees are more likely to violate the code of ethics.
- Stealing is up from 9% to 12%.

#gone

"Read the Bible. Work hard and honestly. And don't complain."[3]

Billy Graham

I once heard John Maxwell say, "Leadership is always the problem and leadership is always the solution". If bad work ethic and substandard ethics in the workplace bother you, then, as Gandhi said, "Be the change you want to see in the world." Change starts with you and me. If we want to see better work ethic in your workplace, then we need to have a good work ethic. If we want to see ethical behavior rise, then we need to be ethical employees. Be a good steward, do the right thing. Be a different kind of worker.

Just this week one of the girls in our church was driving to an event with a woman who had been in prison for many years and had recently been released. When the topic of work came up the woman who had been in prison talked extensively about how her boss at her new job was so impressed with her because she did all of her tasks with such excellence and efficiency. The boss had never seen such quality work in such a short amount of time or the mindset of using all working hours to be so productive. She smiled as she told the story and said, "For years I worked in prison being paid 14 cents an hour, and now I'm getting $8 an hour my boss will get his money's worth." She is so grateful to have work! And she gets it; if she is being paid to do something she is going to do it right the first time. If we all worked like her we would have the happiest bosses in the world and would be promoted right, left, and center.

I don't know if we think about this very often, but the Bible talks about how God rested from His work. God worked! God rested. We have been created in His image. It is good for us to work! It is also good for us to rest from our work. Work brings out the best in us. Many times it forces us to connect with people we normally wouldn't choose. It puts us in environments where we can grow and learn new strengths and skill sets. As a child, maybe the word "chores" had a bad connotation and as you grew up that turned into an allergy to work.

The Bible has much to say about work!

#biblesays

"Take a lesson from the ants, you lazybones. Learn from their ways and become wise! Though they have no prince or governor or ruler to make them work, they labor hard all summer, gathering food for the winter."

proverbs chapter six verses six to eight

new living translation

"So, my dear friends, listen carefully; those who embrace these my ways are most blessed. Mark a life of discipline and live wisely; don't squander your precious life. Blessed the man, blessed the woman, who listens to me, awake and ready for me each morning, alert and responsive as I start my day's work. When you find me, you find life, real life, to say nothing of God's good pleasure. But if you wrong me, you damage your very soul; when you reject me, you're flirting with death."

proverbs chapter eight verses thirty-two to thirty-six

the message

"The wicked man does deceptive work, but he who sows righteousness will have a sure reward."

proverbs chapter eleven verse eleven

new king james version

"Better to be ordinary and work for a living than act important and starve in the process."

proverbs chapter twelve verse nine

the message

"Those who work their land will have abundant food, but those who chase fantasies have no sense."

proverbs chapter twelve verse eleven

new international version

"Wise words bring many benefits, and hard work brings rewards."

proverbs chapter twelve verse fourteen

new living translation

"Work hard and become a leader; be lazy and become a slave."

proverbs chapter twelve verse twenty-four

new living translation

"Lazy people want much but get little, but those who work hard will prosper."

proverbs chapter twelve verse twenty-four

new living translation

"Wealth from get-rich-quick schemes quickly disappears; wealth from hard work grows over time."

proverbs chapter thirteen verse eleven

new living translation

"All hard work brings a profit, but mere talk leads only to poverty."

proverbs chapter fourteen verse twenty-three

new international version

"Put God in charge of your work, then what you've planned will take place."
proverbs chapter sixteen verse three
the message

"Appetite is an incentive to work; hunger makes you work all the harder."
proverbs chapter sixteen verse twenty-six
the message

"Slack habits and sloppy work are as bad as vandalism."
proverbs chapter eighteen verse nine
the message

"Good planning and hard work lead to prosperity, but hasty shortcuts lead to poverty."
proverbs chapter twenty-one verse five
new living translation

"Despite their desires, the lazy will come to ruin, for their hands refuse to work."
proverbs chapter twenty-one verse twenty-five
new living translation

"Observe people who are good at their work – skilled workers are always in demand and admired; they don't take a backseat to anyone."
proverbs chapter twenty-two verse twenty-nine
the message

"Don't work yourself into the spotlight; don't push your way into the place of prominence. It's better to be promoted to a place of honor than face humiliation by being demoted."

proverbs chapter twenty-five verses six and seven

the message

"Work your garden - you'll end up with plenty of food; play and party - you'll end up with an empty plate."

proverbs chapter twenty-eight verse nineteen

the message

"Committed and persistent work pays off; get-rich-quick schemes are rip offs."

proverbs chapter twenty-eight verse twenty

the message

"On the seventh day God had finished his work of creation, so he rested from all his work."

genesis chapter two verse two

new living translation

In the NKJV Bible the word "work" is mentioned in 720 verses. Genesis, the first book of the Bible, begins with God's work: the creation of all things.

Many people spend a lot of time working out how not to work when they should just get to work instead. They waste their time and drain themselves of energy trying not to work [at work], and then when they lay their heads on their pillows at night they aren't proud of their days "work." We need to overcome our allergy to work. The best of who we were created to be is on the other side of that! God worked. God created us to work. He created good works for us to do. Work is a part of God's perfect nature. Work is a reflection of His nature in us. When the fall of mankind happened, work changed for everyone. Before the fall, work was all just beautiful, magnificent, creative amazingness. What used to be creative, productive, enjoyable, awe-inspiring fruitfulness has now become work by the sweat of our brow.

Can we still experience creative, productive, enjoyable awe-inspiring fruitfulness? Yes! By working from a place of rest. Rest in the finished work of the Cross of Jesus Christ. Rest in the knowledge that God loves us no matter what we do or don't do for Him. If we can rest in that truth and reality, then we can come at our work from a very different place in our body, soul, and spirit. It's just as important that we remember we do not work for our salvation. We do not earn favor from God by what we do – ever.

One day I was feeling discouraged and didn't know why. I honestly felt like I had somehow disappointed God. This particular day, all I knew was an overwhelming feeling of discouragement. My husband Jonathan noticed that I wasn't quite myself that day, and asked, "What's wrong?" I love my husband. I told him I just felt bad. I felt like I might have done something to disappoint God. He said, "Listen. How much do you love London?" I said, "A ridiculous amount! Off the charts! To infinity and beyond!" He said, "How easy would it be for her to disappoint you?" and I said, "Impossible." And then he said,

"Okay, can we go to lunch?" I thank God for a husband who can set my thinking straight.

If that overwhelming sense of being a disappointment happened to me, it could be happening to somebody reading these pages, too. Please allow that to be an encouragement if you've been struggling. It's not what we do or don't do. God loves you. How much? Off the charts! Do we still have to work hard? Yes. But when we work hard from a place of rest, it energizes us rather than tortures us. We can work from a place of labor intensity or we can work from a place of rest. Laziness is an option for us, but the consequences are not.

A note to all the baristas of the world: life is too short for bad coffee. Okay, servers of the world. Life is too short for bad service. Let's be awesome workers at whatever work is before us to complete! Let's be awe-inspiring to the world around us that's surprised when we do someone else's job, or work late without pay because of our personal spirit of excellence. Just be amazing and let that be your job. Let's work from a place of rest. Let's work as unto the Lord. So how do we work well? I'm going to give you keys of some things I've picked up along the way that have built my work ethic. I'm coming from the place of "I love to work," so if you don't love to work, try to introduce some of these things and they just might change your life.

5 KEYS TO WORKING WELL:

1. Have a high completion drive.

Finish today's work today. You may wonder why your to-do list grows larger ever day. It could be that you allow today's work to roll into tomorrow. Tomorrow has it's own work, so you compound it by adding yesterday's. And then, if you don't get on top of it tomorrow, it rolls into the next day, etc. Work at a pace allowing you to complete urgent and important work on the day assigned, if humanly possible.

#biblesays

"And it is a good thing to receive wealth from God and the good health to enjoy it. To enjoy your work and accept your lot in life—this is indeed a gift from God. God keeps such people so busy enjoying life that they take no time to brood over the past."

ecclesiastes chapter five verse nineteen
new living translation

#gone

"We're here to be worshippers first and workers only second. We take a convert and immediately make a worker out of him. God never meant it to be so. God meant that a convert should learn to be a worshiper, and after that he can learn to be a worker. The work done by a worshiper will have eternity in it."[4]

A.W. Tozer

2. **Be enthusiastic, energetic, and excited everyday.**
   I am a high-energy leader and everybody working with me knows
   they need to be high energy, honest high energy. High energy
   leaders appreciate team not showing up looking like they just
   dragged themselves out of bed. How we present ourselves at
   work tells the world that we are ready to do something exciting!
   We are changing the world! We are going to see people find
   Jesus.

3. **Be creative and produce excellent quality and high
   yield quantity.**
   Take initiative – solve problems – steward well. Don't be so
   pedantic about your excellence that you don't get anything done.
   Sometimes we have to move along a little bit quicker.

4. **Be obedient.**
   Follow instruction and pattern. Don't think you know better,
   because you don't. If you did, you would be the boss! Every good
   boss was trained. They didn't know better when they were a
   trainee.

5. **Don't quit when you're in training for something bigger
   & better.**
   Don't quit when it's hard, because when it's hard, you're in
   training! If you're going to make the maneuver to leave, do it when
   it's harder to make the maneuver. Don't jump from one thing to
   another. I used to jump from thing to thing, but in those days I
   didn't know who I was or what I was doing. Thankfully, at the end
   of the day, God has used all of those jobs and experiences from
   my long, special resume to shape me and train me. I want to
   encourage you to do whatever you can to stay the course. Please
   don't be a quitter. If you are in a dangerous or volatile situation, or

even in a job where you can't pay the rent, perhaps you do need to leave and look for something better. Sometimes we have to be practical. Whatever you do, don't quit when you are being challenged, taught, or corrected. If we learn to embrace all of those things we will surely find ourselves in the role we want to be in eventually.

Some people work in full time ministry as pastors, prophets, apostles, evangelists, teachers, preachers, or champions of social justice. Some people work hard at becoming something they will never find success in. For example, there are only so many Grammy Award winners and Olympic Gold medalists. When it comes to work, we need to get on with what's in our hand, and by making the most of every opportunity – big and small – we will discover our gifts.

Most people, however, work as moms, wives, doctors, lawyers, educators, servers, nannies, administrators, CEOs, baristas, bakers, managers, photographers, teachers, personal trainers, personal assistants, cleaners. All are valid if we work as unto the Lord. It's not only what we do, but how we do it. God receives glory in our going to work life when it's offered to Him, whether we wait tables or preach to masses, whether we wipe babies' bottoms or perform brain surgery.

We need to fix our eyes on Jesus for our going to work life. When it comes to work, we need to stay focused on Jesus. We might not love what we do, but we can love Whom we do it for. That changes everything! So now we have to find a way to do what we love, and still be able to live. The dream would be that you have the job you love, it pays you more than you need, but for most people it doesn't work out like that, or at least not right away.

Young people have time and energy but don't have any money. Adults have money and energy, but no time. Then in the older years, you have time and money, but no energy. It almost seems unfair doesn't it?

#gone

"Pray as though everything depended on God. Work as though everything depended on you."[5]

St. Augustine

#biblesays

"Servants, do what you're told by your earthly masters. And don't just do the minimum that will get you by. Do your best. Work from the heart for your real Master, for God, confident that you'll get paid in full when you come into your inheritance. Keep in mind always that the ultimate Master you're serving is Christ. The sullen servant who does shoddy work will be held responsible. Being a follower of Jesus doesn't cover up bad work."

colossians chapter three verses twenty-two to twenty-five
the message

Experts tell us that people who do what they love for a living tend to live happier, more productive lives. Those who don't love what they do are often made sick by working at jobs they hate. We have two choices: change your job or change your attitude. Hate is not an option. Complaining is not an option. Doing shoddy work is not an option. Find out what you love and get to it!

Listed below are 7 benefits of working for love. This could be a combination, depending on your season in life. Maybe this is your paid job or maybe you have been able to find a paying job that releases you to do volunteer work for the Lord. It doesn't really matter as long as you are applying yourself and doing it for Jesus, and unto Him. Sometimes people find it is easier and a better fit for them to be a barista in their current season so they can serve more and work for the Lord. Other people feel very specifically called to a career, whether it is nursing, teaching, or some other area.

Whatever it is that we do for work, we must find happiness, and joy that is not circumstantial. Following are 7 benefits of working for love:

1. Purpose.

   When you're working for love, you will be filled with and motivated by an incredible sense of purpose. Even if the work that you're passionate about doesn't pay the bills yet, and you have to take on a less desirable job to pay the bills in the meantime - know that God sees and watches everything. So work at that lame job with all your heart. Don't despise it. Bless it instead!

2. Personal connection with what you're doing.

   You wake up in the morning very differently, looking forward to getting to work on something that you actually love.

#gone

"My share of the work may be limited, but the fact that it is work makes it precious."[6]

Helen Keller

3. Productive fruitfulness.

    This comes from working on something that you are passionate about. When we put our gifts and talents to work as an offering before God, we will have something to show for our efforts.

4. Promotion through relationship.

    Usually when you're doing something you love, you are able to connect with other people who are doing what they love and there's a synergy that may find you being promoted.

5. Prosperity in finances.

    We reap what we sow. When we sow hard work with a good attitude of heart and soul, we will reap. When we sow our best efforts as an offering before God, we need to allow for the process of time: seed, time, harvest.

6. Prevention of stress.

    There is a great deal of stress associated with repeatedly doing things we do not like. If we choose to love what we do, we will lose the stress.

7. Psychological strength.

    When you are working for love you are better able to focus on what you are doing now instead of thinking about somewhere else you would rather be.

When you're faithful with what is in your hands, God will give you what is in your heart. I was taught this principle by my pastor many years ago. There's nothing better than that moment when you recognize, "I was born to do this. I would not want to be anywhere else or do anything else." Sometimes we need to figure out how we are going to get paid.

#gone

"We must do our business faithfully; without trouble or disquiet, recalling our mind to GOD mildly, and with tranquility, as often as we find it wandering from Him."[7]

Brother Lawrence

I was talking to my personal trainer and dear friend, Michelle. She is a phenomenal personal trainer, the best I have ever come across in all of my years of being in the fitness industry. She told me about a recent appointment and as she spoke about that encounter, her eyes filled with tears. She said, "I love this. I really love this."

Michelle truly cares about helping others succeed in life, and loves being able to guide people throughout their journey to achieve health and freedom. Does she like lifting up people's weights for them in her role as a personal trainer? Let's be real. It would be helpful if a client lifted their own weights, but I saw something when tears welled in her eyes. I saw just how much she loves helping people. It is wisdom to adopt the idea that if we are able to work, we should be grateful to work. I love that my friend is grateful to work, whether she is paid or not. The spirit of the volunteer loves to work no matter the reward.

I have experienced many miracles in my life when I have sown my best work as an offering before God and He has always looked after me financially. Our work can be so full of purpose, so full of passion. My hope is that you will gain a deeper understanding of your current season, to realize that whatever your work looks like, whatever you're doing – what is already in your hands is really important because it will release what is in your heart.

Having a strong work ethic is a good thing, providing you know when it's time to stop. There have been seasons of my "going-to-work" life where what was required to fulfill my role [sometimes up to 80 hours per week] was unsustainable for my season of life. Although I enjoyed my work and had the personal capacity to meet the professional demands it placed upon me, the pace I was going was not healthy for my children. One of the hardest moments in my "going-to-work" life was to ask if I could work part-time instead of full-time. I came to this decision because I was only putting my kids to bed a couple of nights per week.

This wasn't occasional, it was continual.

I was hoping that those I was serving would see how hard I was working and how hard I was trying, and that they would somehow raise the subject and make adjustments so I could raise the kids I brought into this world. Ultimately I had to take responsibility for bringing the subject to light. I learned through this particular "going to work" season that it was up to me to change my life. It took me some time to find the courage to initiate the conversation. The conversation was difficult, but it was necessary, and fruitful. It took over a year to transition from full-time to part-time because of all the responsibility I carried, but once I transitioned I was so relieved. I felt like I could breathe. I continued to work hard and in my part-time [paid] capacity I managed to give a full 40+ hour work week without any problems.

Sometimes we need to go for a walk around our lives and really assess what we are doing and who we are doing it for. I am convinced of this one thing, people will always ask more of us than God asks of us, and it is up to us to discern the difference. When you take the risk to make the necessary adjustment, you will find God's favor and grace will make up the difference in your life!

My amazing, gracious and very hard-working mother observed my life throughout that bigger than big season, yet she didn't say a word. When I finally made the positive, healthy changes that were essential to the well-being of my children, she finally spoke up, saying, "You will never have any regrets". Wisdom from the wise.

Although I had to walk a different road, a hidden road out of the limelight of "prime time" leadership, I have never had any regrets from that decision. Even when my kids asked me why no-one seemed to know who I was anymore, my kids were beyond happy to have me back. My response to them would always be, "As long as you know who Mummy is, that's all that matters".

Our "going to work" life, whether it is in the corporate world or the ministry world, should never be at the expense of our children. God gave them to us, not as a human shield to excuse us from being involved in what God wants us to do, nor left behind whilst we pursue something we believe God has called us to. God has given us kids to bring alongside of us. Our "going to work" life is their journey too.

I am so grateful to God for a spirit of release and rest over my life that had to come from Him because it wasn't going to come from people. When we are GONE, we enjoy the benefits of working from a place of rest in Him.

"If God is satisfied with the work, the work may be satisfied with itself."[8]

C.S. Lewis

Thank you, Lord God, for giving me the ability to work, to be a worker for You, to be on Your team. Thank you, Lord God, for giving me the ability to understand the deeper meaning of our everyday life, and that I can have significance in whatever it is that I do. Thank you, Father, for a great job with great pay. Father, thank you for helping me remember your principles; that I need to tithe and sow, that I can expect finance to come into my life. Thank you, Lord God, that I can look forward to seeing promotion I have not seen before. Thank you for Your blessing that I have not seen before. And, Father, as I am diligent with what is in my hands, thank you for releasing what is in my heart. I thank you, Father God, for sealing your Word. Let me not be allergic to hard work. Let me love it and embrace it in Jesus' Name.

Amen.

walking around life

to watch – notice – remark – note – keep – observe – assess – perceive

#anonymous

Jesus' hidden years … and yours

"In our sensory-driven world, it is easy to reduce our working definition of 'living' to the stuff we can touch, taste, feel, heat, and see. Easy, but unwise. Such a reduction renders us vulnerable to a deadly form of hopelessness when we experience pain-filled trials or pleasure-less times. Additionally, it leaves us entirely defenseless in temptations of appetite. Jesus did not accept this definition. He believed that living was initiated and sustained by God and therefore could not be measured by the physical senses alone. 'Life is' because 'God is.' We literally exist by the power of God's Word, and if he were to withdraw that Word, all life would utterly perish."[9]

Alicia Britt Chole
Anonymous

Life is beautiful when you look through the lens of GONE.

God invites us to place our sleeping, eating, going-to-work and walking-around life before Him as an offering. These are aspects of our everyday ordinary lives. Now having looked at those other aspects of our lives in previous chapters, let's go for a walk around our lives and see what we can see. For the purpose of self-evaluation and growth, I want you to take a good long look at your life. Go for a walk around – observe your life. We're not trying to take ourselves on an out-of-body experience or anything like that, but when was the last time you actually put yourself in the shoes of someone else who interacts with you? It's interesting when we take a look at our life and observe it, not from the standpoint of ideals, but in reality. If I were to ask you to tell me about your life, you might tell me about the ideal of what you wish your life looked like, or you might tell me about the realities of your life. We need to take a real, close-up look in order for us to take accurate steps forward.

If you have ever played the party game, "Pin the Tail on the Donkey," you will recall the blindfold and the donkey poster. The donkey poster is stuck somewhere on the wall and the child is given a tail and a pin, and that child has to go and pin the tail on the donkey. To have more fun, you spin the child around so their orientation is confused. Everyone watches and laughs until the next child's turn. Eventually, when everyone has had a turn, someone has usually ended up pinning the tail on the donkey. This brings up a point - if we're blind we can't observe our life accurately. When life has spun us all around and we feel confused, we are no longer able to observe our life accurately. The Bible tells us that there are people who, when they walk around their life, can't see their life. Their life is dark, like a shadow. We can't observe life properly when we can't see, and there are none more blind than those who are spiritually blind. We need to ask God to help us see clearly. We need to know where we are so we can see where we're going.

#biblesays

"The people who sat in darkness have seen a great light..."

matthew chapter four verse sixteen
new living translation

Let's walk around our lives and take an honest, unfiltered look. Following are four questions to ask yourself to see how your life is going.

1. Am I "idle" or am I "intentional?"

In Australia there are signs all over that say, "No Loitering." This means that you can't hang out there. If a "No Loitering" sign has been put up somewhere, then that place at some time has been known to be a place where people hang out. We need to make sure that when we are just hanging out that we are not just mindlessly or aimlessly squandering our time; that even in our time spent away from work we are using our time intentionally and with purpose. Idling is the act of doing nothing or no work, and we should ask ourselves the question: are we idle, or are we intentional? When used to describe a person, idle typically carries a negative connotation with the assumption that the person is wasting their time by doing nothing of value.

When a car is turned on, burning fuel, but not going anywhere, it is idle. Idleness in our lives looks like that too. We are awake and coherent, but just burning daylight, letting time and energy go to waste. Idleness is associated with things that are dormant, inactive, unused, or vacant. If we see the picture painted from those words, we can realize it is not what we want out of our lives. We won't come to the end of our lives wishing we had been unused, inactive, or vacant.

The difference between idle and intentional is a choice, a choice to see the value of time and energy in our lives.

It's important to know we can also be idle when we're busy, busy, busy, filling our time and our day with nothing that matters. An example of this is the hamster on his wheel running and running but never going anywhere. He is expending his energy, moving his little body at an incredible rate, but not making any movement forward.

"What we hope ever to do with ease, we must learn first to do with diligence."[1]

Dr. Samuel Johnson

Let's take a walk around our busy, busy lives and look at what it might be like in the hamster's wheel, and make some changes. What is taking up your energy and focus and not producing any movement forward in your life? We need to kiss our hamster wheels goodbye! Let's make a commitment in our lives not to be idle, lazy, sluggish, inactive or sloth-like, in body, soul and spirit.

The opposite of sloth is diligence, which is the virtue of hard work. Benjamin Franklin once said, "Diligence is the mother of good luck."[2] Diligence is the decision to fulfill all of the responsibilities in our vocation or state in life. It is described as a zealous and careful nature in one's actions and work; having a decisive work ethic, budgeting one's time; monitoring one's own activities to guard against laziness.

I present myself as disciplined because I have had to work hard at becoming a woman of discipline. However, it doesn't come naturally to me, so it may not come naturally to you either. At the core of all of us is the potential to be lazy and a desire to take shortcuts, but there are many rewards in living a disciplined life. When I turned 43, I skied for the first time in 25 years. I skied from 9.30am in the morning until 3.30pm in the afternoon with only a 45 minute break. I was on the slopes that whole time. To be very honest, 95% of the reason I ski is for my kids, and only 5% is actually for the love of skiing. I'd prefer to hang out in the lodge. I would be a great lodger. I would be the happiest little lodging queen you've ever known. Give me the hot chocolate, give me the marshmallows, give me the cute outfit! Give me the warm hands and the toasty warm feet! I don't ski for myself. I intentionally choose to spend active time with my kids doing activities they really enjoy.

Are we idle or are we intentional? The good thing about being intentional is that you can also be intentional about your rest. Living with intention doesn't mean we have to be "on" all the time. We also need to be intentional about having some time off. Just be mindful that "time off" doesn't turn into an excuse for "time idly spent."

#biblesays

"Lazy hands make for poverty, but diligent hands bring wealth."

proverbs chapter ten verse four

new living translation

"A sluggard's appetite is never filled, but the desires of the diligent are fully satisfied."

proverbs chapter thirteen verse four

new living translation

"Diligent hands will rule, but laziness ends in forced labor."

proverbs chapter twelve verse twenty-four

new living translation

"The plans of the diligent lead to profit as surely as haste leads to poverty."

proverbs chapter twenty-one verse five

new living translation

Idle is a dreadful way to live - just hanging around, shooting the breeze, doing nothing, bored. We need to make sure that we are never idly wasting the precious time that God has given us.

2. Do I live by "conviction" or do I live by "confusion?"

Conviction is: faith, belief, principle convinced, a strong persuasion. Confusion is dangerous. When you are in a state of confusion or lack of clarity and you don't think that you have options, remember you always have options with Jesus. He will never leave you to choose between two evils. Don't ever sell your soul because of confusion. Be convinced, have a conviction. Confusion is about us being unable to think with clarity or act with understanding and intelligence.

It is vital to take time in making big decisions, especially if circumstances have arisen in life that may have caused us to become confused about something. If something has happened to throw you into a state of confusion and turmoil, now is not the time to make life-changing decisions, no matter how much pressure you may feel. Now is not the time to leave your husband. Now is not the time to think that having a baby is going to fix it. Now is not the time to quit your job, move to a new house, to move the kids – now is absolutely not the time. If you are confused – please don't do anything until you feel a strong sense of conviction that overrides confusion, and allows your decision to align with the Word of God. Be in the company of good counsel. Let this be something you follow through with for the rest of your life. There is no need to walk around confused!

Most people mean well. Even those "special" relatives mean well. Those nearest and dearest friends mean well. It is often the "un-surrendered" friend or family member who will suggest our old life was our best life. We need to wise up.

When you know that the Holy Spirit has given you a clear directive, stay convicted.

#biblesays

"Now faith is confidence in what we hope for and assurance about what we do not see."

hebrews chapter eleven verse one
new living translation

We need to be aware of people who come alongside and try to cast shadows on what the Holy Spirit has spoken into your heart. Conviction leads to peace. Confusion leads to more confusion. Certainly there are times when we need to be rescued from our own poor thinking and potentially dangerous choices. There are times when we legitimately need that kind of intervention.

I'm not talking about a situation where someone is trying to rescue you from yourself and you legitimately need that kind of intervention. We can convince ourselves about any nonsense, but conviction comes through the Holy Spirit. The conviction that comes through the Holy Spirit, if it is true and proper conviction, will be obvious to others. They will see the Holy Spirit is in your conviction. If you're the only one who can see it – then you might be convinced rather than convicted. I never make a big decision without talking to at least five people. Ever. I love the assurance that comes from being surrounded by wise counsel. Sometimes we need help understanding the difference between being convinced and being convicted. That's the purpose that wise counsel serves in our lives.

3. Do I "walk" or do I "wander?"

Do we "mosey" or do we "motor?" There's a great difference between a casual approach to life where we might find ourselves just wandering from here to there, and a much more purposeful approach where we know we are going, with something to do. When we walk around with intention we meet new people, we find new places, we see things in a way we wouldn't if we were rushing; we see the beauty of creation, we walk and pray, we think creatively and we meet new opportunities.

Revelation happens when we aren't rushing. Revelation happens when we aren't wandering – it happens when we are seeking God.

#gone

"A 'No' uttered from the deepest conviction is better than a 'Yes' merely uttered to please, or worse, to avoid trouble."[3]

Gandhi

#biblesays

"I am confident in the Lord that you will take no other view. The one who is throwing you into confusion, whoever that may be, will have to pay the penalty."

galatians chapter five verse ten

new international version

When we stop chasing the wrong things, the right things will find us. Walking around with intention is powerful. Jesus walked around with intention. He walked here and he walked there, but was He ever just shooting the breeze? No, He wasn't. He was intentional about where He walked and why He walked there. We need to live like that and be true followers of Christ. He was intentional in his work and He was intentional in His rest.

Wandering around life unintentionally is dangerous, and can cause us to lose our way. When we wander around life unintentionally, with no compass and no thought of where we've come from, where we are now, and where we're going, we'll get lost. This is when we find ourselves in potentially dangerous or compromised situations, causing us to maybe say, "Oops, how did I get here? Oops, how do I get out of here?"

Consider the life of King David and his encounter with Bathsheba. He might have been standing there, looking out his window, but he went out to wander via his imagination. You can go wandering without leaving your current physical location. Wandering doesn't have to be geographical. You can be physically present at work – where you are supposed to be doing your job, because you are being paid to do your job, but mentally you might have decided to be elsewhere for the day. Praying is one thing; letting your mind wander is another. At work we need to work. If you go to work, do your job and do your best.

When we wander around life unintentionally, we waste time. Do you know how much time you have? You really don't know exactly how much time you have! What a sobering thought! I don't want to sound morbid, but do you know how much time you have? I don't know how much time I have. I'm aware of it. The older my kids get, the more time I feel like I don't have. I'm not talking about time in my day. I'm talking about time left in my life. What are we going to do with it? We can't waste it – it is too precious.

Maybe offense has caused you to wander away from your life's purpose. Maybe you were into something amazing, but now you are upset about something and have decided to walk away. Come back, please! Don't waste your time, or your seed. Stop wandering, come back and get intentional. When we wander around life unintentionally, we waste time and we potentially disconnect in an unhealthy way from important elements in life: relationships, work, responsibility, consistency, and healthy priorities. We need to be aware of our potential to wander. What does the Bible say about wandering thoughts? Take them captive! Don't allow yourself to befriend wandering thoughts that will take you off course.

Wandering can be a wonderful activity in your free time [window shopping, for example]. However, it is very unhealthy as a lifestyle. My husband loves when I go window-shopping. Sometimes I wander through the mall and I shop without spending money. That's his favorite way for me to shop. When I wander through the mall, I motor my walk so I can maximize that time. Everyday – day in, day out - I try to maximize my time because I don't want to miss a moment for Jesus. Wandering around in our free time to do some window-shopping is good as an every-now-and-then activity, but it is not healthy as a lifestyle.

4. Am I "easily interrupted" or am I "easily distracted?"

Can God interrupt us with His assignment? Can people interrupt us with their genuine needs? I say genuine because the neediest people do not usually shout the loudest for our attention. There are people who are always around us and are always in need, like the screamers versus the ones who are silently lying still, at the scene of an accident. Paramedics usually leave the screamers until last. If they are screaming they know they are breathing. The first to receive attention are the motionless silent, as they could very well be dying. We need to be able to discern the difference between God-interruptions and distractions from people who will waste our time to suit their own purposes.

It isn't wise to continually allow just anyone to interrupt us, because there are some interruptions that are wastefully rude. If some people have your number, they'll use it … all the time. They will call on you again and again and again. If people are in genuine need, then help them, but if they are just draining you, you need to establish some healthy boundaries. Love and lead people, but learn to avoid being drawn into problems they need to sort out for themselves. Where there is genuine need, are you interruptible, or are you too easily distracted to hear from God and help people in need? When we let people who are time wasters – distractions – eat up our time then we don't have the capacity to respond to those truly in need.

If you are easily distracted you may be too distracted to hear from God, to see what He needs you to do. If you are off chasing something over "there" you may miss what God has for you to do right "here." Distraction is dangerous. Distraction diverts our attention. Let's go for a walk around our lives and be very real. How well are we able to distinguish the difference between a Godly interruption and something that is a distraction designed to take us off course?

If you have a track record of jumping from one thing to another, ask those around you who know you well and are friends to your destiny. They may say you are easily distracted. Check to see if the diversion you're currently on is bearing fruit. If there is no fruit and just more confusion and time wasted, it's likely you've wandered off on a distraction rather than walked into an opportunity sent by God.

Do you recognize that God will often interrupt us through people He has appointed as leaders over our lives? Many times the growth we pray for, or the breakthrough we need, will come to us through opportunities to serve. But what happens when your answered prayers come in packages you did not expect? Do we push those opportunities away and go back to praying?

#biblesays

"You were running superbly! Who cut in on you, deflecting you from the true course of obedience? This detour doesn't come from the One who called you into the race in the first place. And please don't toss this off as insignificant. It only takes a minute amount of yeast, you know, to permeate an entire loaf of bread. Deep down, the Master has given me confidence that you will not defect. But the one who is upsetting you, whoever he is, will bear the divine judgment."

galatians chapter five verses seven to ten
the message

We need to remember that if we make what is important to God important to us, He will bring what we need into our lives His way. What do you do when one of your leaders calls you and asks you to serve in an area?

So many people respond to their leaders with excuses such as, "Not now, I don't have time. Maybe later." What they are really thinking is, "I can't commit and follow though because I actually have commitment issues." Sadly, when we are not honest with ourselves, and when we are not honest in our responses, we will always try to cover up with excuses. When the phone rings, the Caller ID is not going to say "God." I don't know about you, but I don't want to get that phone call. Your Caller ID is more like to say your boss's name, or your leader's name, but it could be the Lord calling you – interrupting you, saying, "Excuse me, can I please have some of your time because this person in the shelter actually could really do with your story. This person really needs a hug from you." Will we allow ourselves to be interrupted? Or does it always have to be about an opportunity?

Distraction stirs up confusion. An interruption is someone or something breaking in upon action. A distraction is someone or something changing the motion or direction one is in. So you need to ask yourself – are your friends, the people you spend time with, the people you listen to, the people you allow speak into your life – are they the sort of friends who are easily interruptible because God needs them or people need them? Or are they the sort of friends that cause you to get more distracted? Maybe that's why they always call you with a crazy idea.

Sometimes people crave the excitement that distraction brings: a rabbit trail, an adventure, a random story to tell. But what we are really missing when we crave that excitement would actually come to us if we allowed God to interrupt our lives. Then we will have real stories to tell! The kind of excitement you might crave is similar to the story of

Jesus at the well in John 4. The disciples had gone into town to get some food and Jesus has a very pivotal conversation with a woman at the well, one where He reveals who He is and her life and the whole town is changed forever. And what do we find when the disciples return with food? We find Jesus saying He isn't hungry anymore. He was so fulfilled by doing the will of the Father. He says that He has food they know not of. If Jesus was available and open to God interruptions, we should do likewise.

Let me encourage you to watch for God interruptions and make yourself available for them. An interruption is often our best opportunity. A distraction often takes us out of our current opportunity.

You know what would be great? If we didn't spend our whole life working out the issues of our life, and could get on with proclaiming the Good News of the gospel for a world going to hell. That would be phenomenal. Jesus was often interrupted but never distracted. Jesus' purpose remained intact even when his timing and destination was deterred.

As pastors, Jonathan and I are always on call, but we do have a day of rest. The Bible says we are to have a day of rest. God rested, so we also have a day of rest, but on that day of rest, we are most certainly interruptible. Did Jesus heal on the Sabbath? Yes. Religious people don't like to be interrupted on their "day off." Did Jesus catch rest when he needed rest? Yes. We need to understand that there is the world's structure, which, for the majority of people, is to work Monday to Friday. That is not the scriptural structure for followers of Christ. As Christians, we need to work out our own rest in whatever we do. We need to let our calendar and our big fat schedule be interrupted by Jesus' purpose. Jesus had the opportunity to be distracted from God's timing for His life, God's authority at work in His life, and God's perfect will for His life. Jesus had opportunities to be distracted, just like we do today.

#gone

"He [Jesus] has a right to interrupt your life. He is Lord. When you accepted Him as Lord, you gave Him the right to help Himself to your life, anytime He wants."[4]

Henry Blackaby

Remember, when Jesus came to earth, He came as a man. Human. He carried all of our human-ness and all of his God-ness, so He could have easily been distracted and He had to make sure He wasn't. Jesus could have been distracted from God's timing for His life, just as we can. It's distraction and lack of revelation that says to God when He calls, "Not now, Lord. I'm not ready for ministry – I'm just going to have a little playtime now. I am not ready, I will do it in my 40's. I'll get more serious about living my life for You later."

I love to see young people on fire for Jesus. I love to hear young people talk about Jesus. We need to talk about Jesus. We must be looking for vital signs, because it's not playtime. The intentional life does have playtime in it, but it's not "either/or" – it is "and." But the intentionality is that we are always open – because this is our life. This is our Romans 12 life. It is laid down as an offering before God. And in it, it is always about Jesus.

God's authority at work in Jesus' life could have been a problem. Imagine if Jesus had actually wanted to do His own thing? He was a human being. What if He decided that His will was more perfect than God's will? This is not just about Jesus and God – this is about us and Jesus and God. Where do you see yourself? Is God a compartment, or a department, or the head of an institution to you? Is God up there in the clouds? Where is Jesus? Is He in your heart? Is He seated at the right hand of the Father? Is He walking around like in the time of the gospels still performing all those miracles? And where are you? Where do you fit? Where do I fit? I don't ever want to see myself as being separate from Him. Ever. You need to walk around your life. When you walk around your life, where are you? Where do you see yourself? Romans 8 says that sin cannot separate me from His love. So if I keep following Him, up close and personally, then I'm less likely to keep doing anything to disappoint Him, or make me feel separated. How closely are you following Jesus? If He stopped, would you run into the back of Him? Are you that close to Jesus? You have permission to take up all of Jesus' personal space. Where do you see yourself? This is such an important question to answer, because guilt and shame serve as barriers keeping you from feeling that love, and stop you from feeling included. Living with guilt and shame will cause you to become more distracted when you leave any kind of space. Make a decision today to close the space between you and God.

3 NAVIGATIONAL GOALS:

1. Be at the right place.

2. At the right time.

3. With the right people.

Being in the right place, at the right time, with the right people means that it's not all about us, and our favorite friendship group. If you are interruptible, God can lead you to be in a completely unfamiliar place, at a time you didn't ask for, with people you don't know - but if it is a God appointment, it's essential that you be there. Being in the right place, at the right time, with the right people is all about "kairos" [God's appointed time] meeting "chronos" [earth time]. How do we get there? Maybe you have walked around your life while reading this chapter and you've realized you've been hanging around, confused and distracted. Maybe you've allowed distance to come between you and Jesus and now you want to find your way back to Him. He is right here, right now, and He never moved away from you. You had your blindfold on, and your friends spun you around like you were playing "Pin the Tail on the Donkey". It's okay, because you know what God loves to do? He loves to open blind eyes. God loves to give us spiritual revelation that will change our direction for the rest of our life.

#biblesays

"And we know that God causes everything to work together for the good of those who love God and are called according to his purpose for them."

romans chapter eight verse twenty-eight
new living translation

As you honestly and accurately observe your life right now, maybe you're in pain because you feel overwhelmed by your circumstances. Let me assure you, everything that happens is either God-sent or God-used. There is no waste. None.

That means we win, because God is on our side, working on our behalf. It doesn't mean everything will make sense when you wake up tomorrow, or that you have to be clever enough to sort it all out. It does mean if you are in God's hands you can trust that He will put everything into the right place.

Please don't be overwhelmed by what you don't understand. God has been God for a long time [eternity] and He is not overwhelmed with your situation. Our world today has many people who have trusted God and allowed Him to use the unspeakable things they have been through to bring hope and freedom into others' lives. Not to mention our heroes of the faith who went through incredible hardships, but what we find when we look back at their stories is an all-powerful present God, and no wastage. He doesn't send us misfortune, but he will use our misfortune for His glory.

We need to pray and ask God to help us stay focused on Him and His purpose for our everyday, ordinary, walking around lives. Let's walk around with God! Do you know that God enjoys your company? I love to think about Adam and Eve walking around with God in the Garden of Eden. Can you imagine the relationship, the freedom, the overwhelming sense of completeness they would have had? There was no idle wandering or distraction in the Garden of Eden. Can you imagine walking around in that place? We need to find that in this life.

I find Jesus to be the most amazing teacher because He shines His light on the most complex of situations and breaks them down for us, showing us a way forward that is much less complicated than we might have anticipated. He makes things simple, bringing peace and clarity to our lives.

#biblesays

"Here's what I want you to do: Find a quiet, secluded place so you won't be tempted to role-play before God. Just be there as simply and honestly as you can manage. The focus will shift from you to God, and you will begin to sense his grace. The world is full of so-called prayer warriors who are prayer-ignorant. They're full of formulas and programs and advice, peddling techniques for getting what you want from God. Don't fall for that nonsense. This is your Father you are dealing with, and he knows better than you what you need. With a God like this loving you, you can pray very simply. Like this:

Our Father in Heaven,

Reveal who you are.

Set the world right;

Do what's best - as above, so below.

Keep us alive with three square meals.

Keep us forgiven with you and forgiving others.

Keep us safe from ourselves and the Devil.

You're in charge!

You can do anything you want!

You're ablaze in beauty!

Yes. Yes. Yes.

In prayer there is a connection between what God does and what you do…"

matthew chapter six verses six to fourteen

the message

We need to learn to walk and pray with God. This connection is everything. Who is God and where do you see Him? Who is Jesus and where is He? And where are you? We have a visual picture of all these components. Who is the Holy Spirit? Where is He? Let's walk and pray with God.

10 WALK AROUND WITH GOD PRAYERS:

1. **Dear God … Our Father in Heaven.**
   Remember God is in Heaven: all knowing, all-powerful, always present. God is not at lunch. He is not disinterested or ignoring you. He does not favor one person over another.

2. **Dear God … Reveal who You are.**
   Revelation is greater than resource. When God reveals who He is in the midst of where we are going, it changes everything. When we can see, it makes sense. Just when we thought we were in the wrong place, with the wrong people, at the wrong time – revelation shows us – no it's the right place, right time, right people. Stay.

3. **Dear God … Set the world right.**
   Allow God to sort people out. Be careful not to become distracted by non-fatal relational drama. Pray and ask God to intervene.

4. **Dear God … Do what's best - as above, so below.**
   Yield your will to God's will. Believe in faith to walk in the freedom Christ has provided, and exemplify it for others. It is good for us to ask God to "do what's best." We don't always know what's best. Have you ever been thankful for a prayer that God did not answer?

5. **Dear God ... Keep us alive with three square meals.**

Remember, God is our provider. Please don't panic or behave as though you don't know Him. If my children were to start panicking about not being fed, it would show they don't know me, because I love to feed my kids great meals everyday! God is the most amazing provider of food on planet Earth. It's His great pleasure to feed you! This prayer is all about what we need in our natural everyday, ordinary lives. We need provision for shelter, for clothing, for food. We need to know that He is our provider and we can trust Him. Let's thank Him for what we do have, and not complain about what we don't have.

6. **Dear God ... Keep us forgiven with you and forgiving others.**

Let's keep short accounts. Be sorry and say sorry to God [confess our sins] daily. The meaning of repentance is that you turn around and determine in your heart you'll never do it again. And if you find yourself doing it again [because we are human and imperfect], you turn around, say sorry, and you decide never do it again. If you do it again, read Romans 7! The important thing is to be sorry first and say sorry to God. Forgive those who say sorry, and all others who don't. Forgive all of them.

7. **Dear God ... Keep us safe from ourselves, and the devil.**

Take responsibility for your actions – we can't blame the devil for everything. We do however have an active adversary [the devil] who wants to take us out, and we are not ignorant of his devices. I often pray to ask God to help me move out of the way of my own life. We want to fix everything but some things only God can restore.

8. Dear God ... You're in charge!

    God is not blind, nor deaf, nor passive. He watches over everyone
    and He watches over everything that happens. The good. The
    bad. The ugly. He will bring justice. We need to bring Jesus!
    When we simply cannot work out how to solve a problem,
    because it is beyond our control, that's when we need to
    remember our God is in charge.

9. Dear God ... You can do anything you want!

    When we give God room to move, He will. God will never make it
    worse for you when you give Him room to move. I don't know
    why we have an issue with this. Why do we say things like, "God,
    you can have anything you want, but don't touch my finances.
    Even though they are a mess, I don't want you to touch them."
    Sometimes we say, "God, you can have whatever you want, but
    don't take that guy out of my life 'cause he's cute... and he has
    money." We need to trust God and pray prayers like, "You can do
    anything you want, and I will trust You to bring someone else into
    my life if that guy doesn't love You like I know I need to love You."
    We should say, "I trust you Lord. I don't have what I need right
    now, but I do have seed. Here is my seed."

10. Dear God ... You're ablaze in beauty!   Yes. Yes. Yes.

    Our God is more magnificent than any earthly treasure. Jesus is
    more valuable than any earthly opportunity. The Holy Spirit is
    more treasured than any earthy relationship. This is a wonderful
    prayer because it's a prayer of praise. We can come to God with
    our requests – He doesn't mind. It's beautiful when we come to
    God and just say, "Thank You. I want to tell you I love you and I
    want to praise You." Think of God the Father. A father loves being
    appreciated. A father loves it when his kids say, "Dad, you're the
    best! I want to let the world know that you are the best dad on

planet Earth. Thank you! Thank you! Thank you!" We can say to our Heavenly Father, "Father God, You're ablaze in beauty. Yes, yes, yes!" What a crescendo of prayer. These are the words of Christ instructing us how to pray a simple prayer.

Go for a walk around your life. This life is too precious for us to allow it to just slip away. We need to look at our life. We need to be very careful not to walk away from responsibility because our activity and our motion is everything. We need to walk toward God's purpose and run away from evil. That's what the Bible says. Run from evil, flee from it, hate it and don't engage in it. Leave it. Don't leave it as an option for later. Run. Flee from it.

People are watching us as we stay at our post. They are watching our commitment or, they are watching us waiver. Please don't walk away from the post that has been entrusted to you. What would it take for you to walk away from your post, from that place that God has you currently? Whatever it is that might cause you to walk away, deal with it, and say, "I will not walk away, Jesus. I will not walk away unless the Holy Spirit tells me to and everyone else says 'Yes, that is God.'" Do not walk away from your post. The devil wants you to leave your post. He wants you to turn your back on everything that is important so there will be fatalities. We need to make a decision that we will not allow offense to rule our lives.

If we allow ourselves to become offended and then we stay offended, we will lose heart and we will lose face, and the next step will be, sadly, walking away. We each have a post we are called to stay at, whether it is a position of leadership or ministry role, or a job where you are responsible for the safety and wellbeing of others. For example, in a hospital environment, there must always be a nurse or doctor on duty, watching over the care of each patient. If they were to walk away, a patient's life could be in danger.

#biblesays

"[Staying at Our Post] Companions as we are in this work with you, we beg you, please don't squander one bit of this marvelous life God has given us. God reminds us, I heard your call in the nick of time; The day you needed me, I was there to help. Well, now is the right time to listen, the day to be helped. Don't put it off; don't frustrate God's work by showing up late, throwing a question mark over everything we're doing. Our work as God's servants gets validated—or not—in the details. People are watching us as we stay at our post, alertly, unswervingly . . . in hard times, tough times, bad times; when we're beaten up, jailed, and mobbed; working hard, working late, working without eating; with pure heart, clear head, steady hand; in gentleness, holiness, and honest love; when we're telling the truth, and when God's showing his power; when we're doing our best setting things right; when we're praised, and when we're blamed; slandered, and honored; true to our word, though distrusted; ignored by the world, but recognized by God; terrifically alive, though rumored to be dead; beaten within an inch of our lives, but refusing to die; immersed in tears, yet always filled with deep joy; living on handouts, yet enriching many; having nothing, having it all."

one corinthians chapter six verses one to ten
the message

On a ski trip with our family one winter we decided to take five-year-old London up on a chairlift on what would be a reasonably difficult run for her – a green run.

London had been in ski school for the day, and we happened to run into her and her group with 30 minutes of ski school left for the day. Last year she had ridden the chairlift a lot and loved it, and so we asked her if she would be going up on the chairlift again. With only half an hour left of ski school, the instructor told us there wouldn't be enough time for it, and London was so disappointed, she even shed a little tear!

Seeing how important it was to London, I said, "Baby, don't worry – Mummy will take you on the chairlift!" We hopped on the chairlift, and as we approached the top we said, "Okay London. Get ready." In a split second, my baby girl had fallen off the chairlift and gone under. Not forward, but under, and I could see her little chair go over the top of her. We were freaking out, and the chairlift operator didn't do anything to help – she had walked away from her post. She had walked so far away from her post, in fact, she could not even run back in time to stop the chairlift.

Fortunately, my husband Jonathan was on the seat behind us, on his own. He for whatever reason wanted to take the "rear guard" [he is very protective]. Thank God! He was on the chair by himself – which is also a miracle, because normally they have four people loaded up. He saw what just happened. He saw that there was no way the chairlift operator could get back to her post. London was sliding down backwards, under the chairlift. Jonathan, with his snowboard on, was about to slam into her with it. I'm being a little dramatic, but that chairlift was about to seriously injure her. Needless to say, at this point, everyone who could see what was going on was screaming. The supervisor in the cabin with his own set of controls was also not watching. Jonathan had to make a decision. As he jumped off the moving lift to avoid running over her, his snowboard landed on her legs, because otherwise he would have taken her out. Then the crew started screaming at Jonathan, "Get off her! Get off her!" and I started calling out at them, "That's her father!" I tried to reach London, my skis still on, trying to climb up the mountain. The staff member who left her post was negligent. The supervisor who was supposed to be supervising her post was negligent. The whole situation was terrible, and no one was sorry.

Thankfully, London was fine. She hurt her ankle a little, which was already sore from skiing. The ski staff was not kind, they were not gracious, they didn't seem to care, and made it worse. They took far too long to get anyone to help us get down the mountain. They sent a medical person who traumatized London further by telling her he was going to take her to see a doctor at the hospital in an ambulance. London was so frightened that she was practically crawling up Jonathan's body, away from the medic, frantically saying, "I'm not injured! I lied, I'm not injured!" My husband had some really intense things to say to that man right then. All of this could have been avoided if the lift worker had just stayed at her post. Imagine what might be avoided by choosing to stay at our post.

All I want to say is: if you're at a post – just think about it - if the Lord has put you at a post and you turn your back and you turn away, you don't even know what's going to happen. Please don't go. Don't leave there. Stay at your post. There might be someone headed your way soon whose life is going to change if you don't move. Can you stay at your post?

Take a walk around your life and observe not only the intention of your heart, but also observe the actual attention of your life. When our intention and attention align, you will find yourself GONE.

Life is truly beautiful when we surrender.

GONE.

#pray

Father, help me be a committed, loyal follower of Your Son Jesus. Help me to obey your Word, and help me to always be led by Your Holy Spirit. Help me stay at my post through good times, and difficult times. When offenses come and when opportunities come, allow me the grace to stay in place."

Amen.

#biblesays

"So here's what I want you to do, God helping you: Take your everyday, ordinary life—your sleeping, eating, going-to-work, and walking-around life – and place it before God as an offering."

romans chapter twelve verse one

the message

place it

to put or set in a particular place, position, situation, or relation

#anonymous

Jesus' hidden years ... and yours

"People of all ages experience hiddenness. In fact, the poor navigation of hidden years later in life has ended more than a few souls' previously sweet legacy in bitterness. The challenges we face throughout the span of our lives certainly change, but our need for nurturing the discipline of self-control never expires. However, perhaps no other space in life is more critical for the development of self-control than the hidden years of our teens, twenties, and thirties. In these early anonymous seasons, God graciously grants us the opportunity to wrestle with our appetites 'before' other lives are at stage, to struggle with our passions privately before moral collapse affects the innocent publicly. There, in the unphotographed spaces of hidden years, when we are not 'calling the shots' or 'taking the heat' or 'on the frontlines' or 'in the spotlight,' self-control has the opportunity to grow, slowly and steadily, layer upon layer, until all that inner strength fuses together and creates something indestructible."[5]

Alicia Britt Chole
Anonymous

To be GONE is to be fully surrendered, and I believe that the fully surrendered life is our best life. Until we fully surrender, we won't experience the amazing life God wants to give us, the amazing life that He can only give us once we have fully laid down our old life.

We need to look at our lives and ask, "Is my life my own?" Yes, you could say your life is your own in the sense that God gave you and me free will to do with our lives whatever we want. However, we must also understand our lives are not our own, now that we have a relationship with Jesus Christ. When we accepted Christ as our Savior, we put Him in charge of our lives – we made Him Lord of our life. Now He gets to call the shots. Whenever we try to pick up our old life again, we will soon see our lives fill with confusion, stress, and struggle.

Consider this: we are God's masterpiece. We are not our own masterpiece. We've been created anew in Christ Jesus. We have to understand that placing ourselves, as it talks about in the Message translation of Romans 12:1, is an act of grace. This GONE message is a message of grace. It is not about us putting ourselves somewhere in order to earn God's favor.

The placement of our lives is an act of grace, and we need to get our heads around that fact. Let's place our lives. Let's think about this as we ask ourselves these questions:

1. Where have you been?
   - past life, past years

2. Where are you now?
   - body, soul, spirit, geographically

3. Where are you going?
   - 5 years, 10 years, 25 years from now

#biblesays

"God saved you by His grace when you believed. And you can't take credit for this; it is a gift from God. Salvation is not a reward for the good things we have done, so none of us can boast about it. For we are God's masterpiece. He has created us anew in Christ Jesus, so we can do the good things He planned for us long ago."

ephesians chapter two verses eight to ten

new living translation

If you were to place yourself somewhere, where would you be in 5 years time, 10 years time, 25 years time?

For some aspects of our lives, there should be no change except for growth in that one place, but for other parts of our lives there should be astronomical growth and change and movement and expansion and surprise. Do you ever think about where you want to be in 5 years? Do you think about how much you want to grow in 5 years or 10 years?

When we place our lives before God, we place our whole lives before God: our body, soul, and spirit. The scripture talks about us doing that as a living sacrifice, which means you are still alive while you are being placed. It means you are more alive than ever. All of your emotions are alive, all of your body is alive, and of your spirit is alive. This means that you're going to be faced with feeling pressure when you're being placed. You're going to be faced with being put in situations you might prefer not to be in. A living sacrifice is very different from a dead sacrifice. A dead sacrifice doesn't feel anything, doesn't know anything. You can carry a dead sacrifice anywhere and they are fine – they won't feel anything. Our old self is dead, but the new self that has to get on with it is very alive. So we are placing our alive new selves before God.

We are God's masterpiece. We are not our own masterpiece. We have been created anew in Christ Jesus. We are not our old selves and we have to see ourselves placed in this masterpiece. I don't know if you've ever been to an art museum and seen any beautiful masterpieces. Picture yourself somewhere in the masterpiece, important in the plan of God. There is nothing pretty about a dot on its own that you can't see. We're not meant to be independently off the page. We're meant to be part of this amazing tapestry of grace, this amazing masterpiece God intends for us.

This moment of surrender we have been contemplating throughout this book is about our everyday, ordinary, eating, sleeping, going to work, walking around life, and now we are going to place our lives. It's the ultimate maneuver we can make. It's the full stop or period at the end of our story, where we've understood that all God requires from us is our everyday, our ordinary, our eating, sleeping, going to work, walking around life, and we just need to "park it."

"Parking it" or "placing ourselves" is an act of grace. It's an attitude of our hearts. Every single time we place ourselves before God in this way, we are placing ourselves in the line of duty. If you know anything about warfare, you'll know what it looks like to be in the line of fire. Being in the line of duty puts you in the line of fire. If you're a spiritual leader, then you'll definitely find yourself under fire. This is because the devil is trying to put you "out of place." To combat this, you'll need to step up and deal with anything that could move you, things like offense, burnout, or financial stress. What is it that could move you out of the line of fire? In our next chapter, you'll get equipped to handle the line of fire, because that line of fire is the rightful place for a life laid down in surrender.

You might be wondering at this point, how it is that we went from talking about our everyday lives and ended up talking about the line of fire. Don't worry. The fact is we can handle it. It's okay, because God has given us weaponry to be able to withstand attack. We need to understand the devil loves to pick off spiritual leaders.

We are saved by grace to do good works. We are not saved by our good works, and we don't earn grace. In our church, we do a lot of good works. We do a lot of good in our community, but none of that is to earn us brownie points in heaven. All of those things are our literal response to a relationship with God. We don't need to do anything to receive salvation except receive the gift Jesus Christ has already prepared for us. This is why Easter is so important to our faith. I was recently explaining Easter to London. I had given her the Easter message one night, and wanted to do a recap the next morning. With kids you need to revisit the explanation of important events each year, because each year their ability to comprehend increases. A three-year-old will understand something differently than a four or five or six-year-old. London's level of comprehension is now is quite mature, so that morning I asked her what Easter was about. I was waiting for her to give me the Good Friday message, or perhaps the Easter Saturday message. We have a party on Easter Saturday for our family, because we know what is coming on Sunday! Resurrection! I was surprised to hear London's answer regarding the meaning of Easter. That morning she told me it was all about the Easter Bunny and chocolate eggs! No problem with the Easter Bunny and no problem with chocolate Easter eggs. We just need to ensure that Easter is all about Jesus, first and foremost.

God has a plan and a purpose in place for our lives. When we place our lives, God places our lives. When we give Him our lives, He gives us our best life. It is a beautiful exchange.

It isn't healthy if all we want in our lives is to be consoled. We're graced to be more than that. We should be the consoler. When people come to you with their problems, I hope you are able to realize your role is not to be somebody that goes to everyone else with your problems, looking to be consoled. Hopefully you are able to realize you should be beyond that now, that God has graced you in your laid down, GONE life, to be the consoler. That is a big shift. Sadly, some spend their entire life wanting constant consolation.

Let's take a few moments to look at the word "place." It's an interesting word. The word place has everything to do with position.

- Position
- Posture
- Place

The action of placing our lives is about surrendering control. This is not surrender of self-control. We very much need self-control in our sacrificial-living life, but we don't need to retain control of the steering wheel of our lives.

#gone

"Lord, make me an instrument of your peace, where there is hatred, let me sow love; where there is injury, pardon; where there is doubt, faith; where there is despair, hope; where there is darkness, light; where there is sadness, joy. O Divine Master, grant that I may not so much seek to be consoled, as to console; to be understood, as to understand; to be loved, as to love. For it is in giving that we receive. It is in pardoning that we are pardoned, and it is in dying that we are born to Eternal Life. Amen."[1]

St. Francis of Assisi

If we continually insist on taking the wheel, we are saying to Jesus, "You can save me, but You can't lead me." Until Jesus is both Savior and Lord, we will keep grabbing the steering wheel of our lives.

Sadly, many people talk about Jesus, while actually living largely un-surrendered lives, and Jesus is nowhere near being the Lord of their life. In more secular nations – Australia for example – people tend not to talk out of both sides of their mouth when it comes to Jesus or Christianity. There, most people are either saved and fully integrated into their Christian life, or they're not. Here in America, many people talk about Jesus, but will happily tell you they are the lord and king of their own life, as though there's something right or justified about that. We need to get back to Bible and back to basics. We need to understand if Jesus is going to be Savior of our lives, then He also needs to be Lord of our lives. For this to happen, we need to give up control of our lives, and the antidote for control is, surrender.

When we surrender control of our lives to the Lord, ultimately, we allow Him to rearrange the furniture of our lives. Does anyone else have a tendency to be a control freak, or just me? In my home it bothers me if a lampshade is not straight, if a towel is not straight, if a chair has been moved, or if a pillow has not been fluffed, [and if I acquire one more pillow in my house, it's going to become a fulltime job fluffing all those pillows!]. There is a particular way I like to arrange everything, and if someone was to come into my house and shuffle it all about, mess with my current arrangement of furniture, then I might say something, or I might just get on with putting it all back the way it was, which is often what I spend my time doing.

Does it drive you crazy when someone touches your stuff, messes with your arrangement? It's actually a good illustration for us, because we know how all of a sudden that can cause us to become undone if someone messes with our stuff. And when God wants to do that with our whole life, no wonder we love "Jesus the Savior" more than "Jesus, Lord of All." We are grateful for Jesus the Savior who has ensured our place with Him in Heaven one day. Some are less comfortable with Jesus being Lord. We are all good with Jesus having our lives in Heaven, but can we be all good with Jesus also having our earth-lives too? Being GONE is all about surrendering our lives to Jesus for both Heaven and earth.

In Australia we have a magazine called "Home Beautiful." Here it's called "House Beautiful." Many people have created their own magazine in their imagination – it's called "Life Beautiful." We can get out our "Life Beautiful" and say, "I'm going to have a beautiful life, and this is how it's going to look: I'm going to have this many kids by this age, and I'm going to have this much money in my bank account, and my husband is never going to swear at me - he's going to be the nicest person on planet Earth and we're going to fly around the world at least five times a year. We're going to retire when we're 39 and that's going to be our Life Beautiful. And church! Oh yes, we'll take our kids to church - when we can. That will be our "Life Beautiful"." It looks very different when you actually lay your life down and say, "Okay Jesus, where do You want me now? I'm placing myself in Your hands, and You place me wherever You need me for the rest of my life."

If we think about furniture being our lives, how many times have we done some crazy thing in order to create change in our lives, in order to have some control in our lives? Perhaps we changed where we live, changed jobs, changed where we went to church, changed friends, changed our car, changed our clothes, changed our name – we didn't really care what we changed, we were just determined to change, change, change, in order to have some kind of control.

We do lots of things that represent this subject of rearranging the furniture of our lives because we can't deal with it being settled. We can't deal with it being given over to God, so we just keep working it and working it.

I have someone very dear in my life that is addicted to shopping.

It might sound funny at first, but it's a serious issue. She'll buy the same pair of shoes in ten different colors, and the shoes are over $400 per pair. Clearly something is not right there. You've heard about drug lords pushing drugs, but what about storeowners pushing shoes? Shouldn't the store employees be saying to my friend, "Are you sure you really need ten pairs of those?" instead of "Yes! They're all so beautiful!" This person with the shopping addiction is doing what they can to rearrange the furniture by buying more shoes, but for all the change she creates, she never gets closer to living the life she truly longs for. Control addicts are simply never satisfied.

We have to ask ourselves, are we willing to live this fully surrendered life before God, or do we have to control every single little thing that happens? We can spend the rest our lives simply rearranging the furniture of our lives, or we can allow God to create a masterpiece with our lives. We are saved by grace to do good works. We are not good by doing good works. When we relinquish control, we gain freedom in living right.

HOW DO WE PLACE OUR LIVES?

- To place is to:
    - Put or set in a particular place, position, situation, or relation.
    - Put in a suitable place for some purpose.
    - Put into particular or proper hands.

- When we place our lives:
    - We set ourselves into a particular place, position, situation, or relation before God.
    - We put ourselves in a suitable place for God's purpose.
    - We put ourselves into God's hands for His particular and proper use.

Can Rearranging Furniture be Obsessive-Compulsive Disorder?

"Most people rearrange their furniture, but for people with OCD, it can become an obsession. People with OCD are often obsessed with order. Order means stability to a person with obsessive-compulsive disorder, something they're lacking on the inside… This means they're seldom satisfied with how they carry out a task, so they keep redoing or rearranging it in the hope of getting it "right". In actuality, their constant preoccupation with order, symmetry and cleanliness hides a deeper anxiety and inner turmoil, and their repetitive actions help to direct their mind away from their fears and insecurities. Constantly rearranging furniture can be an obsessive-compulsive disorder trait. The act of moving furniture around gives a person with OCD a way to avoid confronting deeper problems and keeps them from having to face anxiety and fear head on. Instead, they find some degree of solace in the simpler act of changing the furniture."[2]

Article by Dr. Kristie Leong
Edited by Diana Cooper 2010

- When we surrender our lives:
  - God sets us into particular places, positions, situations, and relationships.
  - God puts us in suitable places for His purpose.
  - God put us into particular and proper usefulness for our lives.

There are some things we need to set in concrete, rather than Jell-O, otherwise we will end up rearranging the furniture again. We must do what we can to eliminate our ability to keep switching up our life because we want to control our life. When we place our lives, we put ourselves into a suitable place for God's purpose.

How do you picture yourself before Jesus? I start off by picturing myself before Jesus with my face on the ground – I'm at his feet. I don't see myself as eye to eye with my Savior, unless he lifts my chin up and pries my eyes open. We are to set ourselves at his feet, but we're actually placed in his hands, so we don't stay at His feet. The death of the old self happens at his feet, but the life happens in His hands. There is something that happens at the altar. We say to God, "I'm done. I'm GONE." And then what happens is this placement is into God's hands. There's a process involved! If we try to put ourselves into God's hands without first coming to his feet, we're not dead yet! We return to rearranging the furniture! Some of us need to change the picture we have in our heads of where we are in relation to Christ. We have to see ourselves correctly. When we live our lives GONE, we are fully surrendered and ready for use by God.

When we place our lives, God sets us into particular places, positions, situations, and relationships. Have you ever found yourself in a particular place, situation, or group of people where you thought to yourself, how did I end up here? It's not always going to be glamorous, it's not always gong to feel good, but we understand once we have put ourselves in His hands, that if He has sent us somewhere to do something, we just need to get on with it.

I can remember the first time I was invited to speak in a women's prison in Adelaide. I was terrified, not of the women, but of myself, and feared I would have nothing to say. We arrived at the prison on a Saturday morning, and apparently this was the very first time the facility had ever provided a common area where women from General Detention could come together with women from the Life Skills Unit. The Life Skills Unit is not a halfway house. It's part of detention, but the women there live in an area where they can cook for themselves and wash their own clothes. They're there learning skills that will help them when they're released.

The pastors who invited me had been visiting the prison for eight years, and they have a wonderful relationship with the staff and inmates. They have had favor to get into the prison and interface with the women because they provide beautiful makeovers to the grounds and buildings. This prison is one of the most rundown places I've ever stepped foot in. It looked, felt and smelled like something in a third world country. Thank goodness this place was finally getting a makeover.

When we were on our way to the prison, I felt it necessary to tell the pastor something. I said, "I want you to know don't think I have anything to say, and I'm not joking. I feel extremely shy. Not insecure, just shy. I don't want to be patronizing, and I don't want to minimize, but really, I've got nothing to say. I just wanted to tell you that." The Pastor said, "Ah, don't worry, just tell your story!" Then I thought, "Tell my story, tell my story... okay, but which part?" I didn't say that to him, but these were the thoughts racing through my mind.

When we arrived at the prison we were met by a prison guard, I will refer to as "Mrs. Happy Pants" at the front gate. She was more miserable than any of the prisoners. Our presence was bothersome to her, as she didn't believe the prisoners deserved any encouragement for their future. As we walked in we were told that because this was the first time they had brought the Living Skills girls and the general detainees together, they didn't think many people would show up to our meeting. At these events, the church provides lots of delicious cakes and treats, entertainment including dancers and singers, and then someone shares a short message.

The meeting that day was voluntary – none of the prisoners were being forced to attend, and in order to attend, both groups were strip-searched on the way in and on the way out. These women allowed themselves to be strip-searched twice to come to a church service because they were so desperate for relationship, and wanted to see the same people every time. When they showed up, they were looking for familiar faces. This experience impacted me forever. What's our excuse when it feels too difficult to come to church because it's raining, or because the kids are being naughty on the way, or we're feeling tired?

I want to share something so you can put yourself in my shoes for a minute. We pray prayers like, 'God, send me, use me!' Then He does and we realize, "I'm so inadequate for this task." It's in our weakness that His strength is made perfect in us. I was having the ultimate weak moment – I thought, "I have nothing to say to these women!" I was sitting in the front row, thinking, "The best thing that I can do today is to just be a pastor to these women. I just need to give them the full weight of the gospel in me, and deliver it with maximum love. I don't need to try to be their best friend before I speak to them."

As I sat in the front row, I noticed a girl who had just shown up and was now at the back of the room. As I looked over my shoulder and saw her, and I said, "Thank you Jesus - she is why I am here today." And then within five minutes I looked over my shoulder again, and there were 75 women there! 25 women had come from the Living Skills Unit, and then there were about 50 general detainees. Half a dozen people from the team had come up to me and said, "When you get up there and start talking, don't worry if the women stand up and smoke, or if they talk to each other while you're speaking. They tend not to sit. Don't worry about it. It's not you, it's just how they are." I said, "No worries. I'll talk as if they're paying full attention. They can take whatever they like away from what they hear me share today. It's fine." My time to speak finally came, and when it did, I felt numb. As it is, I'm not a confident speaker. I'm a reluctant speaker. I have never said, "Give me the microphone! I want to speak. God has destined me for platforms." I've prayed, "God, deliver me from platforms!" So at that moment I felt physically numb. When I started to look into the eyes of the women there, I melted. Yet, because of the presence of the Holy Spirit, in a split second I went from having a deep sense of "I can't do this!" to "I was born for this!"

I started to tell them my story, and had been thinking about the TV show "Law and Order." The show always starts with a crime scene, and then it goes back to it and explains how the whole thing happened. I felt it would be good for me to start with the crime scene story of my life. They had given me 20 minutes to speak, but I decided I was only going to take 15 minutes, because I wanted the women to like me and not hate me for speaking too long – so I finished early.

Not one of the 75 people moved during the entire time I was speaking. I'm sure they must have needed to get up to have a cigarette, but not one of them moved. It was amazing. That was not because of the gift on my life, but because God placed me there! I sat in the front row and said, "God, why do You have me here? This is the most uncomfortable place I could be." But when I stood up I knew why I was there, and I felt something incredible.

In Luke Chapter 4, we see an account describing the time that Jesus stood up in the temple and read from Isaiah 61, saying, "The Spirit of the Lord is upon me, because He has anointed Me." The spiritual weight that was on Him – I felt that same weight when I stood before those prisoners. I'm not talking about my own weight; I'm talking about the weight of Jesus in me as I stood there.

#gone

"Tells rebellious men that God is reconciled, that justice is satisfied, that sin has been atoned for, that the judgment of the guilty may be revoked, the condemnation of the sinner cancelled, the curse of the Law blotted out, the gates of hell closed, the portals of heaven opened wide, the power of sin subdued, the guilty conscience healed, the broken heart comforted, the sorrow and misery of the Fall undone."[3]

A. B. Simpson

All I was doing was standing in the right place at the right time, doing the right thing, surrendered.

At that point, I knew I had crossed over, having accomplished what I thought I could never do. I felt a sense of relief. My biggest concern had been that I didn't want to say anything that was going to make life harder for these women. My prayer was that if I was going to say anything, "Please let it help and not harm." My message that day, by the way, was about "Peace" – on how to have peace with where the women were right then. I simply shared the good news Gospel.

At the conclusion of our meeting, we were invited into a high security area. I told the Pastor, "I want you to know that I've done what I came here to do, and I'm okay to not go into the other part of the prison." No one was listening to me, though. The lady in charge said, "Okay, we're going into the high security area now." We had no clearance to go in, but the prison staff said, "We'll take the pastors in there, and no one else, and we've got to be quick." I was herded into this high security area, and we passed through one heavy security door after another. Each door made a loud noise as they were slammed shut and locked behind us.

As they escorted us toward the library, I said to the Pastor who was walking ahead of me, "By the way, I'm here, but I'm not talking. I've got nothing to say. I had nothing to say before, but now I've really got nothing to say. Can you please help me?" He didn't even turn around. He just said, once again, "Oh, you'll be fine." Mrs. Happy Pants was the one who walked us into the library and locked the door behind us. I looked at the faces of these women. I saw beautiful people who had just made some really unwise decisions. Even though some areas of the judicial system are not right or even fair, these women were given as many chances as possible, but they still made bad choices because they didn't know any better.

Amazing grace is available to each of us. Great grace abounds when we are GONE.

#gone

"Amazing Grace, how sweet the sound, That saved a wretch like me. I once was lost but now am found, Was blind, but now I see."[4]

John Newton

I couldn't believe we were locked in a library with these seven women. It was only by God's grace I was not terrified to be in that room with seven women who were separated from the rest of society because of crimes they committed. Naturally speaking, I'd be the worst person to send in there! But the Spirit of the Lord is upon me, and there I was, in a high security prison with seven prisoners.

The Pastor spoke first. He has such an amazing way of putting everyone at ease. Then, the coordinator announced, "Now Pastor Di is going to share her story, because she shared her story so beautifully earlier with the other group." I shared more of my story with that group of seven than I did with the 75.

One of the women in the group had walked into the room, her hair dripping wet, as if she had come straight from a shower. These women did not have to come to this gathering. They came because they wanted connection. Can you imagine how hard it is to be in an environment like that? They would just be faced with themselves all the time. Then imagine them coming in to meet with four pastors! It was hugely confronting for them! This girl with the wet hair kept pushing her hair in front of her face as if she had some sort of nervous condition, and her head was hung low. I had given these women Part A of my story, which was the crime scene, and then I gave Part B, which was the story of how I got out of the crime scene situation of my life. By the time I finished speaking, this girl was doing the same nervous combing of her hair with her fingers, but now in the opposite direction! I could see her eyes, and they were bright! Then she spoke up! This was not a group therapy session, and she didn't have to say anything, but she said, "I just want to say thank you for your story, because your story is my story, but I've got 14 kids, and I didn't get help."

I want to encourage you to take a fresh look at the gospels and look at all the people Jesus said we need to reach out to. We live in a selfish world and we can be consumed with any number of things that don't matter. We can be consumed with how much money we don't have and how stressful our finances are. We can be consumed with good things like our children and their college careers and even sports.

All these women want is connection. If we don't care, who will care? If we don't go, who will go? I'm so excited our church is now engaged in regular visits to Chino Women's Prison in Southern California. Every month I take a small group of women with me and we meet with around fifty women prisoners who have been there, on average, for twenty-five plus years. We teach them the "Mirror Mirror" course on self-esteem and identity, and we focus on helping them develop a sense of freedom from the inside out. Most of these women are doing life without parole because they murdered their abusive spouse. They have known pain on the outside, and pain on the inside. And now we have an opportunity to place ourselves in their world to bring a message of freedom and hope. I always weave my own personal story into words I share with these women, and so often they will speak to me afterwards, saying, "Your story is my story, but I didn't get help like you..."

We all have a story that can help others. What's your story? Where have you found yourself placed by God? Out of our comfort zone, and out of our own control zone, will we allow ourselves to be placed or will we say, "No one tells me what to do, ever!" Will we do everything we can to work out how to get out of helping someone? If God has put us in that situation, maybe it's about our future. Maybe it will bring you into everything you've ever dreamed of. The opportunity to help people will always come to those who are willing to place their lives in God's hands.

Can we truly say these three things to the Lord?

1. Make me, change me, grow me, Lord.
2. Choose me, select me, send me, Lord.
3. Help me, guide me, use me, Lord.

#biblesays

"For 'Everyone who calls on the name of the Lord will be saved.' But how can they call on him to save them unless they believe in him? And how can they believe in him if they have never heard about him? And how can they hear about him unless someone tells them? And how will anyone go and tell them without being sent? That is why the Scriptures say, "How beautiful are the feet of messengers who bring good news!"

romans chapter ten verses thirteen to fifteen
new living translation

When I lay my life down, God picks my life up. When I lay my life down, God becomes the new custodian of my life. When I lay my life down, it is His to do with it as He sees fit. When I lay my life down, I am fully surrendered to a greater life. When I lay my life down, I am fully surrendered to a higher purpose. When I lay my life down, I am fully surrendered to an eternal goal.

THE PURPOSE OF OUR PLACEMENT:

1. To bring good news.

    To walk into any room with grace, truth and peace. If you're going to visit someone in a hospital, don't take your worry shoes with you! Don't say, "I'm so worried about you!" That's the last thing a person needs. Put your peace shoes on. Take peace into the room and be someone who brings peace, wherever you go!

2. Be sent by God.

    Anytime, anywhere.

3. Use your voice.

    Find your words, share your heart.

4. Share salvation.

    The Gospel is good news! To love, serve, give and forgive.

5. Lead people to Jesus.

    The purpose of our placement is to lead, pray, love! Maybe you won't be the person to seal the deal, but our job is to lead people toward that goal.

Will you allow God to send you wherever He wants you to go? As we close this chapter, I want to share with you what I believe matters most when we place our lives, it's important to know what matters most to God when we are giving Him our lives.

Ask yourself some questions:

1. Am I: Industrial or Relational?

   In Luke 10:38 we read the story of Martha and Mary, It's a classic story about the kitchen versus the sitting room. We need to spend more time sitting, and then from a position of sitting with Jesus, we move on to the kitchen. Both are valid postures, but one needs to be stronger than the other. Our motive and methods matter to God. Either we are consumed by the industry of ministry or we are consumed by Him.

2. Am I: Acceptable or Unacceptable?

   In Genesis 4:2-5, we read the story of Cain and Abel. This is a classic story about an acceptable offering versus an unacceptable offering. Cain and Abel both brought an offering to God, but one was acceptable and one was unacceptable. The value we place on God matters to God. If we don't place value on God when we present our lives as an offering to Him, then there is no value to Him. God is either first or last in our lives. It's our choice to make.

3. Am I: Authentic or Imposter?

   Some people are simply litigious. They might not be a lawyer, but they're argumentative and they like to win. They want justice, no matter the cost. Authenticity says that God will work justice as He sees fit. The two mothers that we read about in 1 Kings 3:16-28, are part of a classic story about the fight over a baby. Solomon discerns who the real mother is by her willingness to give up the baby rather than cut him in half. The authentic mother would not fight with the imposter – she walked away because she knew that that baby would be cut in half. The imposter mother didn't care if the baby died – she was happy for each of them to get one half of a dead baby. We need to be careful about what we argue over. The way we place our problems before God reveals the authenticity of who we are and our trust in Him.

4. Am I: Generous or Stingy?

    God loves a cheerful giver – so our whole attitude towards giving matters to God. It's possible for us to give but still be stingy. When we're generous, it's a heart attitude and the amount doesn't matter. Our whole attitude towards giving – our time, talent and treasure – matters to God. Stingy people live stingy lives but givers love to give.

5. Do I: Trust or Doubt?

    The story in Acts Chapter 5 about Ananias and Sapphira is cautionary, and scary. It's a classic tale of placing a partial offering, reluctantly, and then somehow expecting God will not see that! What happened to these two people? They were struck dead! And In the New Testament, too! The story shows us that our integrity matters to God. Our motives matter. Our authenticity matters. It all matters.

At any point, and at any time, this subject of GONE will bring a division of opinion. And it's not going to bring a division of opinion made up of people inside church versus outside church. In the Amplified Bible, John 10:19 says, "Then a fresh division of opinion arose among the Jews because of His saying these things." The division of opinion is always going to be within the church. You may be feeling right now that you would prefer to call the shots of your life rather than allowing God to do so.

#biblesays

"Remember: A stingy planter gets a stingy crop; a lavish planter gets a lavish crop. I want each of you to take plenty of time to think it over, and make up your own mind what you will give. That will protect you against sob stories and arm-twisting. God loves it when the giver delights in the giving."

two corinthians chapter nine verses six to seven
the message

#gone

"Gratitude is an offering precious in the sight of God, and it is one that the poorest of us can make and be not poorer but richer for having made it."[5]

A.W. Tozer

The day we left Sydney, Australia on a one-way ticket with our four kids, and leaving many loved ones behind, including my beloved Mum and Dad and my only sister Kathy, was a day that we purposefully placed our lives and destiny in God's hands, not only for us but also for family. The day we moved our twin boys into two different colleges in two different states, was a day that we purposefully placed their lives and destiny into God's hands, not only for them but also for us. When we place our lives in God's hands purposefully, we can expect God to fulfill His promises. There may be moments of grief, and of course tears, when you say goodbye to one season, but then joy comes when we know our future is going to be brighter than our past.

There is a point to the placement of our lives:

1. To bring everyone we possibly can to Heaven with us.
2. To introduce them to a life of Heaven on earth in the meantime.
3. To glorify our Father in Heaven.
4. To love and follow His Son, Jesus.
5. To be obedient to His Word.
6. To be led by His Holy Spirit.
7. To hear Jesus say, "Well done, good and faithful servant."

Each of us has a choice. There will always be a division of opinion when it comes to our surrender, which is why we need to make that decision ourselves. We need to have an unchanging conviction, and we need to deal with anything that's going to move us, and we need to do it for the rest of our days.

Will you surrender all?

Will you be GONE for God?

#biblesays

"[Jesus speaking], "I am the good shepherd; I know my own sheep, and they know me, just as my Father knows me and I know the Father. So I sacrifice my life for the sheep. I have other sheep, too, that are not in this sheepfold. I must bring them also. They will listen to my voice, and there will be one flock with one shepherd. The Father loves me because I sacrifice my life so I may take it back again. No one can take my life from me. I sacrifice it voluntarily. For I have the authority to lay it down when I want to and also to take it up again. For this is what my Father has commanded". When he said these things, the people were again divided in their opinions about him."

john chapter ten verses fourteen to nineteen
new living translation

#pray

Father, I thank you that this revelation of surrender is something I can enjoy on earth. What a privilege it is to be on Your team! I now know there is more of a role that I can play, which is not just to receive salvation, but when I receive this amazing gift of placing my life before You – this is an act of grace. Thank you, Father, that I can spend my earth-life loving You, serving You, expanding Your Kingdom, loving people, representing You, knowing You. I want to represent You well. I don't want to represent anyone or anything better than we represent You! Father, make me, mold me, guide me, lead me. Whatever is going on inside of me, whatever selfish things surface within me, please help me stay at my post. Help me to always focus on people who need me. Help me focus on the cause of Christ. I surrender Father. I am GONE. In Jesus' Name I pray.

Amen.

my
now life

#gone

SEASON

DEFINITION: acclimate, accustom, anneal, climatize, discipline, fit, habituate, harden, mature, prepare, qualify, school, steel, temper, toughen, train.

CONCEPT: preparation.

the dictionary

the meantime

the period of time between two things, the period of time between now
and when something is supposed to happen

The meantime.

I am deeply sentimental. I'm sentimental about a lot of things, but I am mostly sentimental about people – I collect people. I love thinking about all the people God has brought into my life, and how rich my life is because it is full of people. I'm very sentimental about people, but I'm also sentimental about certain things I own. I drink out of the same mug everyday. My "One Year Bible" I read everyday is a precious possession. I once left it behind at a hotel I had been staying in. I remember calling the hotel and asking very politely for the manager and telling him there was a priceless article left in the room. The hotel sent the head of security to the room - for my "One Year Bible!" They found it and put it in a safety deposit box for me! I drove back up to the hotel and was so relieved to able to get my "One Year Bible" back!

Another little sentimental possession we have is an hourglass I gave to my husband, Jonathan. It sits on top of a sideboard dresser in our bedroom. This hourglass is completely confronting. I have it right here and I've turned it upside down as I've been writing to you. In this short space of time, so many grains of sand have already passed through the hourglass – time is passing before my very eyes.

We have six children. Two of them are still at home. Life is busy, sometimes hectic and always awesome! Sometimes I just wonder about all that God has done in our lives and what He wants to do in our kids lives. Our youngest daughter, London Eternity loves to play with this very special hourglass. Little London will often come into our bedroom and go over to the big sideboard dresser; straight to this beautiful hourglass and she'll turn it upside down. Every time she turns it upside down I think to myself, "Oh no, don't do that!" It makes me want to cry to see her playing with the hourglass! I don't mind the fact that she's playing with it, she's only 6 years old, and to her it's a toy. She does not yet understand what it means and does not grasp its significance. When I see her play with the hourglass I am reminded of the fact that we had a child in our latter years, and I ask God to keep us healthy and strong, so we can live to be 100+!

As time goes on and as we grow, we should look at the hourglass with a deep sense of purpose and significance, and understand how important it is that we don't just flip it, or be flippant with it. We need to realize with every grain of sand that goes down, we can't ever get it back again. Time is passing, and time is valuable. All time is valuable. All time is meaningful. When we aren't experiencing highlights in life, we need to gain appreciation for the meantime. Not one day of our life should be wasted in a holding pattern hoping that time will pass.

The meantime is actually where we spend most of our time. Not the special events or highlights in life. We can't go from one event to another, and think what happened in between is insignificant or doesn't matter.

I recently gave some helpful advice to one of our girls at church who was soon to be married. She was caught up in all the detailed planning that goes along with every wedding. Some of her plans were coming together really well, while others weren't working out. I assured her that only 20% of what she was doing for her wedding day would actually matter. She told me that thought helped her so much, because ultimately, a wedding day is just one single day out of your entire lifetime of days. Now, that's something to think about for all brides-to-be, Mom's-to-be, corporate giants-to-be! We spend so much energy focusing towards one day, and then what? Then we are faced with the meantime; the meantime before that day and the meantime after that day.

Life is made up of seasons and while they may not seem like it at the time, in the light of eternity those seasons are all so fleeting. I can remember coming to my mother's room on my 3rd birthday and saying, "Where are my pressies, Mummy?" I don't remember very much from between the ages of 3 and 5, but I do remember being 5. At the age of 5 I first started going to Sunday school, and first knew that Jesus was my best Friend. I also vividly remember being 12, carrying a silver cassette carrier around - I wish you could see it! I still have the cassette carrier with all the same cassettes still inside. I told you I am deeply sentimental! Some of the cassettes have really funny names. One tape is called "Family Noises" – I don't even know what that means – it would be so funny to listen to and find out what family noises I might have recorded. There's one tape that is labeled "Funky Mix", and there's also a tape in here that my youth leader gave me, it's the Sex Pistols. I did not like the Sex Pistols, and I did not like that my youth leader gave me that tape, but I do find it amusing now that he did give it to me and that I still have it. I loved my 80's music. I know some people went through a season back in the day where they felt the need to burn all their records, but that was not me. My husband went through that season, but not me. I still love my 80's music and I still listen to it to this day!

When I was a little girl I loved to play. When I was a teenager I became super adventurous and wanted to explore beyond my family. In my twenties I was trying to find out who I was and what I should do with my life. My thirties were consumed with kids and work and family and friends – to be honest it was quite a blissful blur. I'm now in my forties and I have discovered a stride I believe will help me accelerate my purpose for life, for the rest of my life. And I know that my life won't be reduced to "either/or."

I am officially at mid-life and loving it! Forty-five years old. I have energy and experience. I have more wisdom now than ten or twenty years ago and I look forward to wisdom and wonder increasing in my life until I am 100+! I can recall distinctly as a teenage girl wondering what life would be like in my thirties and forties. The good news is, life is better than anything I imagined. My life isn't perfect, but my purpose is an exciting adventure I wouldn't trade in for the world.

Everyday we have a fresh opportunity to maximize our life's purpose, regardless of what season we may currently be in. Our GONE life is always our best life in spring, summer, fall and winter.

Following Are 5 Natural Seasons Of Life:

1. Infancy & Early Childhood

   Children acquire their unique view of the world in the first six years of their life and it's in this season they gain the confidence and curiosity to venture beyond the family.

2. Childhood & Adolescence

   After learning cultural skills and information in early childhood, a dramatic move of the biological clock brings on puberty during this season. These formative years before and during adolescence [ages six to twenty] require the stressful task of molding an identity while the biological and social clocks are out of sync.

3. Early Adulthood [Ages 20-40]

   It's in this season that young adults hear the first of many urgent messages from the social clock: to separate from family, get a job, find a mate, set goals, and face the realities of life. This is a developmental period [ages twenty to forty] of intense social growth, when people make choices that will affect their lives long into the future.

4. Middle Adulthood [Ages 40-60]

   While some people in middle adulthood [ages forty to sixty] have attained their goals and achieved personal command, others have experienced losses that prompt changes in direction. In this developmental season biological and social clocks fade in importance, and the psychological clock has greater influence.

5. Late Adulthood [Ages 60+]

In late adulthood [age sixty and older], the psychological clock becomes dominant as the biological clock begins to winds down. This last **season** of human development is a period when people evaluate the stories of their lives and wonder what they might do to change or add to them.

.... if they have time.

Before we can live the seasons well, we need to know how to read the seasons. We need to know the importance of maximizing our season, whatever the weather, and we need to remember what and Who is constant!

Whether it is summer or winter, weather is the constant.

Whether we are building or dismantling, motion is the constant.

Whether it is a time of war or peace, fighting is the constant.

Whether we are sowing or reaping, time is the constant.

Whether we live or die, eternity is the constant.

Reading the seasons is one thing, living them is another! Theory is one thing, practice is another. Mastering all of them individually is one thing, fitting them or blending them together beautifully is another. We need to create harmony and not clanging, clashing and confusion, regardless of the seasons! And we need to have a vision for our lives so we can be committed to making nothing from something [don't sweat the small stuff] and to making something out of nothing [focus on building your life].

Every season contains a window of opportunity for our future. This season is our current opportunity. Ask yourself some questions:

1. What can I learn in this season that I can't do in any other season?

2. What can I do in this season that I can't do in any other season?

3. What can I give in this season that I can't do in any other season?

#biblesays

A Time for Everything

"For everything there is a season, a time for every activity under heaven. A time to be born and a time to die. A time to plant and a time to harvest. A time to kill and a time to heal. A time to tear down and a time to build up. A time to cry and a time to laugh. A time to grieve and a time to dance. A time to scatter stones and a time to gather stones. A time to embrace and a time to turn away. A time to search and a time to quit searching. A time to keep and a time to throw away. A time to tear and a time to mend. A time to be quiet and a time to speak. A time to love and a time to hate. A time for war and a time for peace."

ecclesiastes chapter three verses one to eight
new living translation

Every season has a window of opportunity. When we look at the many and varied seasons of a human life, we can see both midpoints [highlights] and meantime [everyday, ordinary life].

1. Marriage

Marriage contains seasons of:

- romance and passion as well as bad breath and lost socks
- let me do it for you as well as "do it yourself"
- wrinkles from smiling as well as wrinkles from years
- for richer as well as for poorer
- sickness as well as health
- fear as well as faith

The constant needs to be love. Loving your partner for life.

5 Keys to Living the Seasons Well in Marriage

1. Give your BEST 100% - not 50/50
2. Lower your expectations
3. Increase your tolerance
4. Grow your friendship and commit to growing old together
5. Forgive quickly

Whether the season is summer or winter in your marriage, you can set the temperature or atmosphere.

2. Parenting

Parenting contains seasons of:

- joy as well as frustration
- pride as well as disappointment
- creativity as well as mess
- playtime as well as exhaustion
- fear as well as faith
- The constant needs to be love. Loving your kids for life.

#biblesays

"Love is patient, love is kind. It does not envy, it does not boast, it is not proud. It is not rude, it is not self-seeking, it is not easily angered, it keeps no record of wrongs. Love does not delight in evil but rejoices with the truth. It always protects, always trusts, always hopes, always perseveres. Love never fails."

one corinthians chapter thirteen verses four to eight
new living translation

5 Keys to Living the Seasons Well in Parenting

1. Do not abdicate your parenting.
2. Ask the Holy Spirit to help you.
3. Increase your energy levels!
4. Release them to be adventurous and to always trust God.
5. Make memories.

Whether the season is building or dismantling areas of your parenting, be pro-active. Keep moving forward.

3. Ministry

Ministry contains seasons of:

- clarity and direction as well as silence and uncertainty
- enthusiasm and empowerment as well as boredom and containment
- highlights as well as low lights
- hatch and match as well as dispatch!
- celebration as well as administration
- fear as well as faith

The constant needs to be love. Loving the call of God for life.

5 Keys to Living the Seasons Well in Ministry

1. Be a willing "yes" person when it comes to the call of God.
2. Lose self-imposed boundaries that shrink your life.
3. Be faithful with seed.
4. Get trained, pursue further education, study the Bible.
5. Stay focused and stay in your lane.

Whether the season is war or peace, keep fighting for the Cause. Whatever the season, remain committed to the surrender of your GONE life.

#biblesays

"And let us not lose heart and grow weary and faint in acting nobly and doing right, for in due time and at the appointed season we shall reap, if we do not loosen and relax our courage and faint."

galatians chapter six verse nine
amplified version

4. Money

Money contains seasons of:

- plenty as well as scarcity
- spending as well as saving
- sale time as well as "at no time!"
- abundance as well as agony
- working hard making it as well as playing hard spending it
- fear as well as faith

The constant needs to be love. Loving to give at all times.

5 Keys to Living the Seasons Well with Money:

1. Tithe and offerings are not negotiable. #biblesays
2. Make a budget and stick to it.
3. Be generous on all occasions and remember that money isn't our only currency of generosity.
4. Be creative without spending more.
5. Value a single $1.

Whether the season is seed-time or harvest… keep sowing.

5. Friendships

Friendships contain seasons of:

- friendship building as well as sometimes cutting ties
- distance as well as closeness
- giving as well as taking
- confidence as well as uncertainty
- security as well as insecurity
- fair weather as well as storms
- fear as well as faith

The constant needs to be love. Loving your friends enough to be "tough."

#biblesays

"Bring all the tithes into the storehouse so there will be enough food in my Temple. If you do," says the Lord of Heaven's Armies, "I will open the windows of heaven for you. I will pour out a blessing so great you won't have enough room to take it in! Try it! Put me to the test!"

malachi chapter three verse ten
new living translation

5 Keys to Living the Seasons Well with Friends

1. Be a true friend regardless. Live "the truth in love."
2. Draw your dependency from God not your friends.
3. Be willing to outgrow some friendships.
4. Embrace friends of your call and your destiny.
5. Always love, but keep at arms length one-way, co-dependent, life-zapping friends.

Whatever the season, the Bible tells us we have a friend in Jesus – who is The Faithful Friend of all friends! Whether your season requires you to be a soldier or a builder or both at the same time, always be a lover. The constant thread through our surrendered GONE lives and through all seasons needs to be:

- Loving God.
- Loving people.
- Loving life.

Let's be committed to love.

Notice that fear as well as faith feature across every area [marriage, parenting, ministry, money and friendships]. The one thing that will prolong a hard season is fear. The one thing that will shorten a hard season is faith. Fear and Faith cannot co-exist, so while our season of fear [whether in our marriage, or in our money, or in our ministry] exists, faith will be absent and your season will be a mess.

The Bible tells us the only thing that conquers fear is "perfect love," that is, not us and our ability, but God's love in and through us and our seasons!

When we are GONE, we surrender our right to fear and we commit ourselves to a life of faith, and a life of experiencing His perfect love. We have a dream for our future. We have a dream and we know that God has put it there. What we need to know is God did not put that dream in our hearts to frustrate us. He put it in our hearts to see it fulfilled in our lifetime.

GONE is our starting place. This is where our true-life adventure begins. GONE positions us to be ready for our bigger and better future life ahead. We live GONE [spiritual]. We live surrendered [soul]. We also currently live in our own earth-life reality [body]. So what do we do in the meantime?

Sometimes we may feel stuck in a "meantime season" when it comes to our finances. Maybe you are waiting for a job, waiting to be able to afford a car, or waiting to buy your first house.

When it comes to relationships, maybe you are waiting for your future life's partner. Unless you are called very specially to not have one, you are probably in a meantime season of waiting for one. And then when you do get married, you might find yourself waiting for a baby. We just need to be sensitive to people. If you become pregnant because you "blinked," please remember that it's by the grace of God you are pregnant. Let me assure you of one thing, it wasn't because of your doing, or because God gifted you with fantastic biology or whatever you think it might be. Let's be sensitive to others, because we don't know whom we are talking to, and that person might have been trying to have a baby for many years. For every one person who finds out they are having a baby, there is always another who finds out, for yet another month, that they are not. Sometimes this can be a grueling meantime for people.

We might find ourselves in a physical meantime, waiting for healing to come to our bodies. Let's not confuse a doctor's waiting room experience with God's throne room. When we go to God's throne room, some of us see visually what it is to wait for a doctor to tell us we're going to be well, or that we're going to have a baby. God's throne room is very different. He is our all powerful, all knowing, ever present God. And He's the one we pray to with no appointment necessary.

#biblesays

"While the earth remains, seedtime and harvest, cold and heat, summer and winter, and day and night shall not cease."

genesis chapter eight verse twenty-two
amplified version

The meantime is the period of time between two things, the period of time between now and when something is supposed to happen.

In a history book, a time line looks a little like this…

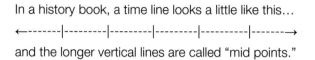

and the longer vertical lines are called "mid points."

These midpoints or "show reel highlights" are what happen in our life at significant junctures. When we're born, for example, or when we start school, get our first job or first boyfriend, or first broken heart. When we get married, have our first, second, third and more children. When we receive our first major promotion, and then, in time, when we retire. When our grandchildren are born and when our great-grandchildren are born. Then we will meet our Savior face to face.

What is in between the "midpoints?" In between our midpoints are what could be called our hidden years or our anonymous seasons. These are the seasons on which we need to have a correct perspective on, because otherwise we'll become obsessed about the next midpoint, the next big event, and we'll end up missing today – we'll miss the moments represented by each grain of sand passing through the hour glass. Our "meantime" is our everyday, ordinary life.

3 THINGS WE SHOULD DO IN THE MEANTIME:

1. Wait Patiently.

We need to wait on the Lord. We need to Trust Him, keep praying and keep believing. The Greek word for wait is "perimeno" which means to endure despite surrounding difficulties.

In our waiting, we do our serving.

In our waiting, God does His working.

In our waiting, we get to know and love Him more.

#biblesays

"Wait and hope for and expect the Lord; be brave and of good courage and let your heart be stout and enduring. Yes, wait for and hope for and expect the Lord."

psalm chapter twenty-seven verse fourteen
amplified version

Servers used to be called "waiters." There's a reason for that. Think about it. In our waiting, we do our serving. In our waiting, He does His working! If we try to work it all out, make it all happen and force a midpoint that is not of God, we may end up creating something in our own strength that we will need to sustain in our own strength. Whatever we strive in our own strength to achieve we will need to continue to strive in our own strength to maintain. The thought of that life is burdensome. Sometimes God answers our prayers at the eleventh hour. Can you wait for, and through, the eleventh hour?

If we can handle the eleventh hour properly, we will experience a midpoint that is graced by God Himself. All too often we'll get to the eleventh hour and give up. In the eleventh hour God is working. That is when the pressure is really on us. If we can just handle our eleventh hour, we will not give birth to our own midpoint and have to deal with that for the rest of our days. In our waiting, He does His working.

2. Get Prepared.

We need to wait patiently, and then we actually need to get prepared! You have nothing else to do! If you're waiting for God to do your midpoint, you might as well get busy in preparations for the next big thing! We should spend everyday preparing for our future.

We can become very obsessed with "our moment in time." God has created us for capacity and if we don't use our anonymous, hidden seasons to de-clutter our lives, then we'll have no capacity to take on what He has for us in the future.

The merchant ship mentioned in Proverbs 31 is not built on the high seas. The merchant ship is built on a dry dock, exactly where it needs to be, in order for it to be built. We don't like being dry-docked because we think God has forgotten us. We may find ourselves wondering where our spotlight is. We want to sail the high seas, but we have to prepare on the dry dock. That season is actually a kindness to all of us. Can you imagine constantly sailing the oceans wide or taking off on a 747 that has not been built properly? Merchant ships are not built on the ocean; they are built in dry docks. There is a reason this scripture is in the Bible for us - God has built us for capacity and we are built during our anonymous hidden years.

We are GONE on the dry dock.

We are GONE sailing the oceans wide.

In every season, and at all times, GONE should be our constant.

What are you doing in your meantime to help you with the next chapter of your life? Maybe you need to go back to school. Maybe you haven't had a role model in your life to help you to understand the power of finishing so you can get to your midpoint of diploma, which is opportunity, which is promotion. We must be good stewards of our time, talent and treasure, because when we jump out of something we have started, we simply get to start all over again in some other meantime.

3. Sow Generously.

We must wait patiently, get prepared and then we must sow generously. At the time of writing, we still do not have a church home [building] of our own. We will have a church home soon, and we are not going to stop believing for our miracle. We will wait. We believe we are at the eleventh hour. My husband's strength inspires me so much! While we may not have what we need right now, some friends of ours who are pastors in Los Angeles recently found their church building, so we sowed a big chunk of seed to them. Why did we do that? We did that because we're still in our meantime and we're waiting for our midpoint. Our meantime helped someone else's midpoint come to pass. Sow your seed. Sow your time. Sow your talent. Sow it, sow it, sow it. Do not invoice it! Sow it. If God tells you to sow something, please sow it.

#gone

"Don't let the fear of the time it will take to accomplish something stand in the way of your doing it. The time will pass anyway; we might just as well put that passing time to the best possible use."[1]

Earl Nightingale

Sowing seed is a midpoint. Reaping harvest is a midpoint. Our constant is time. We will reap what we sow.

- You want a great job?
  In the mean time, volunteer your time.

- You want an amazing husband?
  In the mean time, become an amazing woman.

- You want a baby of your own?
  In the mean time, babysit for others.

- You want a home of your own?
  In the mean time, open the home that you have.

- You want bigger and better opportunities?
  In the mean time, stay faithful with what is in your hands.

Jesus had 30 hidden years and only three years of public ministry. We need to embrace our hidden years, not just acknowledge them, but actually embrace them.

GONE in His spotlight.

GONE in His moonlight.

GONE in His presence.

GOING.

GOING.

GONE.

#biblesays

"Meanwhile, the moment we get tired in the waiting, God's Spirit is right alongside helping us along. If we don't know how or what to pray, it doesn't matter. He does our praying in and for us, making prayer out of our wordless sighs, our aching groans. He knows us far better than we know ourselves, knows our pregnant condition, and keeps us present before God. That's why we can be so sure that every detail in our lives of love for God is worked into something good."

romans chapter eight verse twenty-eight
the message

.

the end

#anonymous

Jesus' hidden years … and yours

"The satisfaction man's approval actually brings is always temporary. I liken mankind's acceptance and applause to rain: we appreciate it when it comes and yearn for it when it is gone, but we have precious little control over its coming or going. Human favor is both fickle and fleeting. Jesus never lived for this longing. But as a man, His heart would certainly have been warmed by acceptance and affirmation and even applause. However, in the realm of longings, Jesus was able to distinguish between what was natural and what was truly needful. Man's affirmation was the former. God's affirmation was the latter."[2]

Alicia Britt Chole
Anonymous

conclusion

"They can take our lives but they can never take our freedom."[1]

Braveheart

As I was contemplating the conclusion to this book, I came across an old, stained Post-It note stuck inside the front cover of my "One Year Bible" [I call it my bedside Bible]. This precious little note has been tucked into my Bible for the past couple of years. "GONE. The book." is written at the top of the note, which goes on to list each of the chapters that you have just read. I'm so glad I kept that little sticky note. That note was the dream seed of the book that you now hold in your hands!

It's good to write down a dream. It's good to write it down after you've accomplished it and tell the story of how you arrived there, but it's also important to write down the seed. It's like putting a stake in the ground. I really want to encourage the dream in you today. Write the dream down.

This book is ultimately all about being completely lost in Christ. Colossians 3:3 [NIV] says that we died and our life is now hidden with Christ in God. When you live your life completely surrendered to Christ, lost in Him, everything that is His is available to you. Instead of trying to be a self-made person, pursuing your own dream, we can allow God to give us a God-dream. We can dream a bigger dream, and can be confident that God won't put that dream in our hearts to frustrate us, but rather that we'll see our dreams come to pass with all His resources available to us to make them happen.

God has put a dream on the inside of every human being. That dream has not been put there by God to frustrate us. It has been put there so that He can fulfill that dream in and through our lives. We need to stay reclined in the arms of our Father – GONE. We need to thank God for making doors open, and for closing other doors. We need to ask God to help us understand the bigger picture of our lives.

He is the Alpha and Omega and only He knows the beginning from the end. Our role is to trust Him completely. Our role is to stay GONE. When we stay GONE, we live in amazing freedom that simply doesn't come any other way. We need to be GONE and stay GONE.

We stay GONE by learning to fight for our newfound freedom. If we don't learn to fight, we will be tempted to pick our old, dead life up again because we don't know what else to do, and then we will try to fight in our own strength. We may even start to compromise on things we said we would never compromise. All of a sudden we find the amazing conviction we once had has become compromised, simply because we don't know how to fight.

We may find ourselves so overwhelmed by external pressure and internal turmoil we think and feel that our only option is to walk away because it is all just too hard. We don't know how to fight the attack of the enemy, so we walk away from our marriage, from our job, from our church, from everything God has given us. I'm passionate about us learning to fight! We are given an armory to fight the enemy. Do not roll over. Do not play dead, and do not compromise. Tell the enemy that he may not touch any aspect of your life! Learn to fight. When we learn how to fight the enemy, we will be better positioned to stay GONE.

Certain things are worth fighting for, and we've got to find our fight. Other things are not worth the bother. We spend too much energy fighting what doesn't matter, and then we're in no state to fight for what does matter.

We need to learn how to stand up and fight for our newfound freedom. If we don't want to be taken out, then we have no option except to be onward Christian soldiers. There is no protection for our backs. We must keep moving forward, so let's make sure we have the armor of God on today. Have you ever picked the phone up to make an angry phone call to someone, but the Holy Spirit has told you not to? He may have prompted your heart so the situation wouldn't worsen. Some battles are not about us. Perhaps you have written an angry email only to have the Holy Spirit tell you to hit delete instead of send. We need to be smarter. If we keep fighting with people, we are unwise.

The Apostle Paul wrote the book of Ephesians from prison …

#biblesays

A Fight to the Finish

"And that about wraps it up. God is strong, and he wants you strong. So take everything the Master has set out for you, well-made weapons of the best materials. And put them to use so you will be able to stand up to everything the Devil throws your way. This is no afternoon athletic contest that we'll walk away from and forget about in a couple of hours. This is for keeps, a life-or-death fight to the finish against the Devil and all his angels. Be prepared. You're up against far more than you can handle on your own. Take all the help you can get, every weapon God has issued, so that when it's all over but the shouting you'll still be on your feet. Truth, righteousness, peace, faith, and salvation are more than words. Learn how to apply them. You'll need them throughout your life. God's Word is an indispensable weapon. In the same way, prayer is essential in this ongoing warfare. Pray hard and long. Pray for your brothers and sisters. Keep your eyes open. Keep each other's spirits up so that no one falls behind or drops out. And don't forget to pray for me. Pray that I'll know what to say and have the courage to say it at the right time, telling the mystery to one and all, the Message that I, jailbird preacher that I am, am responsible for getting out."

ephesians chapter six verses ten to twenty

the message

#gone

"The Christian armor is made to be worn; and there is no putting off our armor till we have done our warfare, and finished our course. The combat is not against human enemies, nor against our own corrupt nature only; we have to deal with an enemy who has a thousand ways of beguiling unstable souls. The devil assaults us in the things that belong to our souls, and labor to deface the heavenly image in our hearts... The different parts of the armor of heavy-armed soldiers, who had to sustain the fiercest assaults of the enemy, are here described. There is none for the back; nothing to defend those who turn back in the Christian warfare."[2]

Matthew Henry Commentary
The Armor of God

Our battle is not with people, it is with spiritual principalities and powers. The only way we will maintain our lives fully GONE is to learn how to fight for our freedom, spiritually. We do this by putting on the whole armor of God.

1. Stand your ground.

We need to make a decision to live for Jesus for the rest of our lives. I have heard story after story where young men and women have achieved the pinnacle of success in their field, and yet their soul is an absolute mess because they don't know what to do with all their success and their gifts. Don't compromise your soul! It is absolutely worthless to gain the whole world, but to lose your soul.

We need to be aware that the enemy will build up a massive portfolio for people in order to take them out. We must learn to stand our ground, no matter where we are along the journey whether we are enjoying the highest heights of success or struggling to see our dreams come to pass. We are to stand because standing is a position of offense.

When we are standing, we are in our offensive position. We need to be on the front foot when it comes to the enemy, not the back foot! The front foot! We are to stand because it is a position of battle or readiness. This may be why the very first piece of armor we put on is a belt, because the belt is a piece of armor that denotes readiness. You wouldn't put your belt on before your pants! Once your belt is on, you are ready to go. Let's look at the belt of truth in greater detail.

2. Put on the belt of truth.

By sincerity, he means the Christian faith. We need truth, and we need sincerity.

#gone

"Truth, or sincerity, is the girdle. This girds on all the other pieces of our armor, and is first mentioned. There can be no religion without sincerity."[3]

Matthew Henry Commentary
Truth

When people look inside our lives, will they see truth? We don't need people to see hypocrisy, or compromise, stress or struggle or anxiety. I recently read that depression is when we worry about our past, and anxiety is when we worry about our future. We are meant to be different. If we are cut open, let us bleed truth.

The belt of truth is positioned to cover our loins, which represent the generations we are responsible for, both biologically and spiritually. We need to gird up our loins – this is an old school term for "we need to wrap it all up tightly." The belt of Truth binds tightly all the other pieces of armor.

The belt is what girds it all securely together, and demonstrates that the believer's readiness for war is truth. Whatever battleground you are in right now – and if you're not in a battle today, then you will be tomorrow or next week, because this is life, don't worry about it. Just be ready to take truth with you. All you need to worry about is truth. You don't need to worry about people making up stories about you. I learned a long time ago not to worry about that. Do people form opinions on what other people say? Yes, they do! But truth prevails. If you stay true to truth, and take truth with you, you are ready for warfare. We only need concern ourselves with truth.

Truth will keep everything tightly together, for us and for our kids [our natural kids and spiritual kids]. Our kids do not need to hear us as mothers uptight about what other people are saying. Too many moms spend time on the phone rehashing what others are saying about them while their children are listening. Let's spare our children. Let's do our children a favor. Let's help train our children to be "truth people." We need to minimize the drama for them and teach them to only be concerned with the truth.

There's no point in wearing a belt if it's not tight enough to hold up what you're wearing. We need our truth to be tight. Truth is our best warfare and enables us to stand in peace. If you know that you know that you know, then you just stand.

#biblesays

"Then he said to the crowd, "If any of you wants to be my follower, you must turn from your selfish ways, take up your cross daily, and follow me. If you try to hang on to your life, you will lose it. But if you give up your life for my sake, you will save it. And what do you benefit if you gain the whole world but are yourself lost or destroyed? If anyone is ashamed of me and my message, the Son of Man will be ashamed of that person when he returns in his glory and in the glory of the Father and the holy angels."

luke chapter nine verses twenty-three to twenty-six
new living translation

3. Put on the body armor of God's righteousness.

The Body Armor of God's Righteousness protects our hearts. It is His Righteousness that covers us. He makes us right with Him. When we're right with Him we get to wear His righteousness. The enemy will tell you you're not good enough, and will try to put you on one guilt trip after another. It's not about what you've done or what you haven't done. It's about what He has already done and you just need to wear Him well. His righteousness covers us. Wearing His Righteousness keeps our hearts from faltering because we have confidence in God's presence and therefore in His Mission for our lives. Without righteousness we are always unsure of our acceptance in Him.

God's righteousness covers our front and God has our back. There is no armor for our back. It is open and exposed, and that is why we have to trust Him. We are free to move forward. Onwards with our purpose, and when opposition is intense, we can just stand. Warfare can cause you to wonder what you did in your past to deserve what is going on. The devil will try to take you out. We must be secure in the knowledge we are in right standing with God so that we don't feel like we haven't done enough and need to be doing something more.

4. For shoes, put on peace that comes from Good News.

We must walk in peace. We must walk in firm-footed stability. We must be prepared for promptness and agility. We must be ready at any and all times to bring peace. It is against opposition that we push forward, but the ground we gain is for the gospel of peace. We must bring Good News! When we live in peace with God, we can walk in peace with others. I can walk down any street with any enemy. I am not in fear and trepidation thinking about bumping into someone with whom I am at odds.

#gone

"The righteousness of Christ, imputed to us, is a breastplate against the arrows of Divine wrath. The righteousness of Christ implanted in us, fortifies the heart against the attacks of Satan."[4]

Matthew Henry Commentary
Righteousness

We ought not to fight with people! Too much energy is wasted fighting with people. Put your peace shoes on and take peace into every situation. You can be the peacemaker.

Wiping the slate clean helps us to live in peace.

We have a lot of kids; they're all very busy, coming and going all the time. One thing I love about them is that they don't fight with each other. They're not perfect by any stretch of the imagination, but we haven't fostered a culture in our home of yelling at each other and slamming the door on each other. We need to be more careful with what our children see and hear.

Be encouraged that it's never too late to start again. Your children will always be happy to see a happy mummy. It doesn't matter what stage they're in right now. Let's be diligent about not affecting our children negatively. When we walk in peace with God we can walk in peace with others.

5. Hold up the shield of faith to stop the fiery arrows of the devil.

Don't let your faith slip. Letting your faith slip looks like this, "Well I don't know if I believe anymore." Your faith is everything! What is not of faith is sin, the Bible says. Don't let your faith slip! The minute you let your faith slip, you are a target. You are a prime target and nothing is shielding you. We need to have this faith that is unseen. Even when it looks like everything around us is going wrong, we don't put our faith shield down and get into it personally. We must get our faith shield back up. What he's talking about is receiving Christ and all the benefits of redemption. Yes, please, I'll hold that in front of me any day. The enemy cannot penetrate that! He can try to shout you down, but he cannot take you out. Shields are something we carry with us. We have to choose to hold onto our shield and not let it go: the choice is in my grip. Let's get a grip, shall we!

#gone

"Resolution must be as armor to our legs; and to stand their ground or to march forward in rugged paths, the feet must be shod with the preparation of the gospel of peace."[5]

Matthew Henry Commentary
Peace

Shields are more mobile pieces of armor, and we can move them to the area where we are being attacked. We can learn to focus our faith and use it like a shield in the areas we may be getting attacked. Your shield is hugely flexible. Let your faith be flexible. Maybe you've seen faith working in healing, but you haven't seen faith work in the area of your finances yet. Maybe you've seen the power of faith at work when it has come to buying a house, but not yet in the lives of your children.

Faith is faith. Where you've seen it once, it's applicable everywhere else. Faith is everything. Do not let it slip.

Understand where your enemy is aiming, and hold your shield steadily there. Tell the enemy to back off. I love my husband. He recently went for a massive prayer walk. When the fiery darts of the enemy are coming in thick and fast, he'll say to me "I'm going out. I'll be back." I'll ask him where he is going and he'll say, "Prayer walk." Two hours later he returns, and the man is glowing like he has seen the Lord himself. You've never seen so much peace walk into a home. If you don't have a husband who does this, then do it yourself. Understand where your enemy is aiming and hold your shield steadily there. Do not put the shield down to pick the phone up. Shields are the key in taking ground and moving forward. They are an outward barrier you can hold ahead of your body as you press forward. This is one of our greatest weapons. Our faith is everything.

6. Put on salvation as your helmet.

We need to put on salvation as a helmet. Salvation means literally to be put back together the way God intended us to be originally. When we say yes to Jesus, all of a sudden broken pieces come together in new life. Salvation as a helmet is so important because it covers our minds. We need to renew our minds and protect our thoughts. Where is the enemy going to attack us first? It will be in our minds.

#gone

"Faith, as relying on unseen objects, receiving Christ and the benefits of redemption, and so deriving grace from him, is like a shield, a defense every way."[6]

Matthew Henry Commentary

Faith

Christians who worry because they're not wearing the helmet of salvation on their heads do not do the Lord any favors. Now, is this hard, to do? Yes! That's why we need armor! Helmets guard our heads: our brains, mindsets, and thought patterns. Salvation functions as a helmet in guarding our minds, and looks like our whole mind being covered by a scriptural expectation of victory.

Having expectation of victory will affect, in everyway, the way we engage and behave in battle. Are you the victor? Last time I checked, you are. Are you the head? Last I checked, yes - you are. Are you going in into a situation confidently, or are you going in confused? Last time I checked, you should be going in confidently.

Helmets protect our heads from head injuries. Head injuries can be so damaging that even after they are "healed" the whole body can still be left immobile, even if all of your other vital organs are in perfect health. Think about it!   We have to protect our head! It affects everything.

7. Take the sword of the Spirit, which is the Word of God.

I am most passionate about this. We should not do a war of words with anybody. We should however do war with the Word instead. To do war with the Word is to remind the enemy – the devil – Who God is and what His promises are. Biblically, this is the only weapon we are allowed to use to attack. If you're using it properly, it will never hurt anyone. There are too many people I know who have been attacked by the misuse of God's word. The Word of God is meant to be used to provide love and hope and healing and reconciliation. It should never to be used as a weapon to hurt. Go to the Word! And if the words you're about to speak are not kind, don't use them! If they're not going to be healing, don't use them. Have you ever wanted to turn back time? Have you ever wished you could take back words that you have spoken? We should always be very careful with our words.

#gone

"Salvation must be our helmet. A good hope of salvation, a Scriptural expectation of victory, will purify the soul, and keep it from being defiled by Satan."[7]

Matthew Henry Commentary
Salvation

"To the Christian armed for defense in battle, the apostle recommends only one weapon of attack; but it is enough, the sword of the Spirit, which is the word of God. It subdues and mortifies evil desires and blasphemous thoughts as they rise within; and answers unbelief and error as they assault from without. A single text, well understood, and rightly applied, at once destroys a temptation or an objection, and subdues the most formidable adversary."[8]

Matthew Henry Commentary
The Word of God

The Sword is the only mentioned weapon we have in our armor, everything else is a tool for defense. Swords pierce, cut, and divide. They are lethal! The Word of God functions exactly like this in our lives. It pierces, cuts and divides lies and nonsense, and it is lethal against the devil. It's not supposed to be a lethal injection to your former friend! We have to apply the force to where the force is due – that is to the enemy.

Swords are only as useful as the skill of the wielder. A good swordsman knows the length, width and weight of their sword. The more familiar you are with your weapon, the greater your ability is to use it. A mature Christian never uses the Word against anyone to harm them. A mature, kind person would never pick up their Bible and bash someone physically or spiritually. Swords must be gripped firmly, so let's get a grip!

We are responsible for the generation we are a part of, as well as future generations to come. If we do not talk about the goodness of God, our children won't know why we go to church and they won't want to come with us! This is about the future! This is about our kids! I'm not just talking about our biological kids, I'm talking about the generation younger than us. We are responsible for the conversations we have, in our car, in our home, at all times. We need to write them on the doorposts so we can remember!

What is the ultimate goal? For me, it is that my children would not look at my life and decide they don't want to follow in my footsteps. I'm not referring to vocation, but I am referring to loving Jesus and following the call of God for their lives. Whatever career path my kids choose, my prayer for them is that they always follow Jesus. Am I grooming my children for the ministry? I don't even know what that means. I am grooming them to follow Jesus. So many of us have a fast track plan for our kids. The ultimate goal for our kids is for them to follow Jesus. We need to fight for the freedom of our surrender, for ourselves and our kids.

#biblesays

"Pray in the Spirit at all times and on every occasion. Stay alert and be persistent in your prayers for all believers everywhere."

ephesians chapter six verse eighteen
new living translation

#gone

"Prayer must fasten all the other parts of our Christian armor. There are other duties of religion, and of our stations in the world, but we must keep up times of prayer... We must pray with all kinds of prayer, public, private, and secret; social and solitary; solemn and sudden: with all the parts of prayer; confession of sin, petition for mercy, and thanksgiving for favors received. And we must do it by the grace of God the Holy Spirit, in dependence on, and according to, his teaching. [I love that. I say that often. How do we pray? Not repetitive, boring, non-engaging fluff. We pray according to the Word, we pray a prayer of faith, and we pray in the name that is above every other name, the name of Jesus. One – two – three. Prayer is not a formula, but those three ingredients make it a rock solid prayer]. We must preserve in particular requests, notwithstanding discouragements. We must pray, not for ourselves only, but for all saints. Our enemies are mighty, and we are without strength, but our Redeemer is almighty, and in the power of his mighty we may overcome. Wherefore we must stir up ourselves. Have not we, when God has called, often neglected to answer? Let us think upon these things, and continue our prayers with patience."[9]

Matthew Henry Commentary
Prayer

#biblesays

"So commit yourselves wholeheartedly to these words of mine. Tie them to your hands and wear them on your forehead as reminders. Teach them to your children. Talk about them when you are at home and when you are on the road, when you are going to bed and when you are getting up. Write them on the doorposts of your house and on your gates, so that as long as the sky remains above the earth, you and your children may flourish in the land the Lord swore to give your ancestors."

deuteronomy chapter eleven verses eighteen to twenty-one new living translation

GONE is a revelation.

When we lay down our lives for the Lord, we are the beneficiaries. When we are completely abandoned. When we are completely trusting. When we are completely at peace. When we are finally surrendered. The natural weight of our lives is transferred to our Supernatural God.

We are GONE.

When we are GONE, we have complete trust, complete rest, complete security, complete peace, complete freedom. The day Jesus became my best Friend, I surrendered to be never the same again. The day Jesus became by Savior, I surrendered to never be the same again. The day Jesus became my Lord, I surrendered to never be the same again.

Jesus my Friend [going].

Jesus my Savior [going].

Jesus my Lord [GONE].

When we are GONE we experience love at a whole other level. Life is a choir made up of many voices, including yours. Join in and sing your part. Let the harmony ring. It may sound strange to you now, but sometimes all you need in life is for someone to sing beside you. One day you're going to look back on smiles and songs you shared with others and smile and sing some more. Because it's sincere human connections – the sharing of a moment – that gives life its best music. Sometimes it happens when you reach out and help someone sing their verse, and other times it's allowing another to reach out and help you sing yours.

God's desire for humanity is that not only would we come to him, but we would come to Him with all of ourselves. Not only that, but we would stay with Him. Not only that we would stay with Him, but we would lean on Him. And this leaning would lead to a deeper sense of trust where we let Him carry us, holding all that we are, trusting Him in everything.

We grow up and leave for College, GONE. We fall in love and get married, GONE. We birth our first, second, third, fourth [and more] baby, GONE. We may lose ourselves for a season in the business of life and much of what really doesn't matter, GONE. We experience the wonder of our children bringing their children into the world, GONE. We arrive at the end of our days, in Heaven's waiting room, contemplating our earth-life that was and eternity to come. One day we will all be GONE. When you stand before Jesus will you know Him as your Friend, will you know Him as your Savior and will you know Him as your Lord? He will know you but will you know Him? To know Him is to love Him. To love Him is to serve Him. To serve Him is to lay your life down for Him.

Going.

Going.

GONE.

I surrender.

No rights reserved.

The end.

#biblesays

"So here's what I want you to do, God helping you: Take your everyday, ordinary life—your sleeping, eating, going-to-work, and walking-around life—and place it before God as an offering."

romans chapter twelve verse one
the message

#pray

Heavenly Father, You are the beginning, You are the end, You are the alpha, You are the omega. You know how it's all going to turn out and if it's not the way it should be right now, then it's not the end yet. Father, I love You and I honor You. Thank you for this armor that You have given me, so I can wear every single piece of it. The fact there is a piece missing in the back means I know you've got my back. Thank you for keeping the enemy away from my life. Thank you for protecting my family, my finances, my friends, my life. Help me remember, Father, that this battle is spiritual. Thank you for helping me fight for the freedom of my surrender. I want to be GONE in your arms and stay GONE in you forever. Help me be a peacemaker. Thank you, Father, for loving so completely. I live to follow you, Jesus, for the rest of my life. In Jesus' Name I pray.

Amen.

in
addition

#anonymous

Jesus' hidden years … and yours

"Submission to God's will and Word brings us face to face with His holiness and our humanity. In the light of God's purity, we realize there are very few things we are incapable of doing. God's Word is like a mirror in that it reveals to us our true nature. That realistic portrait causes us to pause before we belittle others' weaknesses or consider ourselves immune to others' failures."[10]

Alicia Britt Chole

Anonymous

romans theology

the·ol·o·gy is the study of the nature of God

by Jonathan Wilson

#biblesays

"Therefore, I urge you, brothers and sisters, in view of God's mercy, to offer your bodies as a living sacrifice, holy and pleasing to God—this is your true and proper worship. Do not conform to the pattern of this world, but be transformed by the renewing of your mind. Then you will be able to test and approve what God's will is—his good, pleasing and perfect will."

romans chapter twelve verses one and two
new international version

#gone

"Since Jesus has had any of me He has had all of me."

Jonathan Wilson

The book of Romans is considered to be the profoundest piece of all of the Apostle Paul's writings because it describes and establishes the very fundamentals of our faith in such a powerful way. The magnitude of the book is found not only in its content, but in its structure that undergirds and underlines the powerful truths revealed in its pages. In the three major movements of Romans we find a divinely crafted message that gives us a framework of understanding for this masterpiece of Paul's writing. All three of these movements are found in the seed plot and synopsis of the book, Romans 1:16-17.

Movement #1: How the Gospel saves us.

The first eight chapters of Paul's letter to the Romans explain the doctrinal foundation of our faith. The Gospel is the power of God at work saving everyone who believes. We are justified, made right with God, by faith In Jesus Christ not by our good works. In Christ we are dead to sin and alive to God. The wages of sin is death, but the free gift of God is eternal life through Christ Jesus our Lord.

The Road Through Romans

Romans 1 – 8	Doctrinal	Exposition
Romans 9 -11	National	Explanation
Romans 12 -16	Practical	Application

Movement #2: How the Gospel relates to Israel.

In Chapters 9 to 11, Paul writes about the role of the Jew, and the role of non-Jews, the Gentiles, in God's plan of salvation. He emphasizes that the rest of the world had always been a part of God's plan of salvation. God's plan was to reveal Himself to Israel first and then through them to every other nation of the world. The promise to Abraham was that in him all the families of the world would be blessed. The good news of salvation is for both Jew and Gentile.

#biblesays

"For I am not ashamed of the gospel of Christ, for it is the power of God to salvation for everyone who believes, for the Jew first and also for the Greek. For in it the righteousness of God is revealed from faith to faith; as it is written, 'The just shall live by faith.'"

romans chapter one verses sixteen to seventeen
new king james version

#gone

"Romans is the chief book of the New Testament. It deserves to be known by heart, word by word by every Christian."[1]

Martin Luther

Movement #3: How the Gospel shapes our character and conduct.

From Romans 12 to 16 the movement of the book transitions to how the Gospel shapes and changes the way we conduct ourselves in our everyday, ordinary lives. The way we:

- Think
- Act
- Live
- Relate
- Worship

Paul begins with two verses that are pivotal and critical to the application of all he has written beforehand. These verses are Divinely positioned in the very center and heart of the book of Romans and are verses that Paul urges us to place at the very center and heart of our relationship with God. Romans 12:1-2 describe the moment when "we offer our bodies as a living sacrifice holy and pleasing to God" as "the moment of surrender," that moment when the old nature is "gone" and our new nature begins.

Paul urges us to do two significant things, if we are to live in the fullness of the power of the Gospel:

1. We must become living sacrifices.

This is our starting point, offering ourselves as living sacrifices. This is the defining decision in any believer's life. It is the moment of surrender, and until we reach that point of surrender, we will always struggle. We'll struggle with the spirit of God, with what the word of God says to us, with our way of thinking opposing God's way of thinking, with having our way or yielding to God's way.

#biblesays

"For in it the righteousness of God is revealed from faith to faith; as it is written, "The just shall live by faith."

romans chapter one verse seventeen

New international version

Until we surrender, there will always be a sense of disharmony, internal stress and conflict because our lives are out of sync with God. But at the moment we surrender, our lives get into sync and alignment with God and everything changes. That moment becomes the defining moment in setting our course to follow Jesus with all of our heart, soul and mind. When Paul urges us to offer our bodies as a living sacrifice, he isn't talking about:

- Something temporary
  He's not saying you can give your life to God and then go on vacation and take it back again.

- Something seasonal
  Surrender shouldn't be something that is dependent on seasonal convenience.

- Something conditional
  It's a defining decision that we make regardless of the circumstances. We don't need to wait until all the circumstances are right.

- Something emotional
  We don't need to wait until we are "moved by the Spirit." It's not something that is emotional or emotive.

- Something that's vocational
  Surrender isn't only for those who are pastors or in full-time ministry.

Paul is talking about a surrender that is:
- Wholehearted
- Unconditional

- Undiluted
- Unrestrained
- Absolute

I love the way The Message describes this moment of surrender: "place your life before God as an offering." For those who heard Paul's language at the time he wrote this, whether they were Jews or Gentiles, the imagery here was very clear and graphic. It was the image of:

- An Altar
- A Sacrifice
- A Life given

The image of blood being spilled in sacrifices was a common sight in both Jewish and Roman culture. The power and the significance of the image were not lost on those who read and heard these words in the First Century. They knew that nothing was ever the same once a sacrifice had been placed on the altar.

No animal ever got up from that altar.

A life was poured out.

A price was paid.

To someone who was familiar with the Old Testament, many images would have immediately come to mind. Perhaps they thought about Isaac bound on the altar, or maybe of Solomon's offering on the altar when fire fell from heaven and consumed his sacrifice at the dedication of the Temple or of the many other freewill offerings of the Old Testament.

One thing was very clear to Paul's audience, this was not an offering of our lives on the altar for our sins, Christ had already done that at Calvary. This offering was one of dedication and consecration of our lives to God.

#gone

"Whereas the heathen are prone to sacrifice in order to obtain mercy, biblical faith teaches that the divine mercy provides the basis of sacrifice as the fitting response."[2]

Everett F. Harrison

There are 3 things that are central to the laying down of our lives on the altar, as described by Paul:

A. Our will is the key.

Paul is appealing to our will when he says: "Therefore, I urge you, brothers and sisters, in view of God's mercy, to offer your bodies as a living sacrifice." God calls us to make a choice about the way we live for Him, and Paul is urging us to offer our bodies as a living sacrifice if we are to see all that is in Romans 1-8 come to pass in our lives. The word "therefore" is placed significantly before "I urge you" in this verse. Why "therefore?" Because of all that God has done for us, because of all that God has provided for us, because of all the mercy of God.

Therefore, in light of everything God has done for us, including:

- Justification
- Adoption in Jesus and identification with Christ
- Set under grace, not law
- The gift of the indwelling Holy Spirit
- Help in all affliction
- Standing in God's election
- The certainty of coming glory
- The confidence of no separation from the love of God
- Total confidence in God's continued faithfulness
- Offering your body as a living sacrifice

When I accepted Christ as my Savior although it was a deeply and profoundly moving experience, in which I had a literal vision of Jesus, it was not an emotional decision that I made. It began with a conscious decision to seek God. Before I had even prayed the prayer, "God if you are real, if Jesus is the only way, reveal yourself to me," I had made a mental decision, "If I do become a Christian am not going to become a halfhearted Christian."

I was determined if I was going to be a Christian, I was going to be a Christian through and through. If I was going to be a follower of Jesus, I was not going to be a Christian on Sunday and a heathen on Monday. I decided that my faith would be all or nothing. I recall hearing this quote in the early days of my Christian walk: "Since Jesus has had any of me, He has had all of me." I made a decision I wanted that phrase to be what described my life. "Since Jesus has had any of me, He has had all of me."

Paul is saying, "Make a decision, as an act of your will, to let Jesus have all of you." The laying down of our lives is primarily an act of our will. I wonder if we can truly say, "If Jesus has any of me, He's going to have all of me?"

It's significant. Paul says we are to offer our bodies and that involves all of our being, including our flesh which will struggle the most with being offered as a living sacrifice! Paul knew the struggles we all experience with our flesh. In the seventh chapter of Romans he laments, "The things I don't want to do, I do and the things I want to do, I don't do." Which is why Paul urges us as to offer our bodies as a living sacrifice as an act of our will.

The body is a wonderful servant, but a terrible master. Keeping it at God's altar as a living sacrifice keeps the body where it should be! We will still have struggles like Paul, but when we make a decision as an act of our will to offer our lives as an offering to God, it's that decision, that defining decision that changes everything.

The next thing that is central to the laying down of our lives on the altar, as described by Paul is:

B. The level of the surrender of our lives determines the level of God's power in our lives.

What Paul is saying is that if there's no death in our life, there can be no resurrection. If the flesh is alive, kicking and screaming, it's hard to experience resurrection power. We have to master the flesh by a conscious decision to offer our lives as a living sacrifice. The level of our surrender determines the level of God's power in our lives.

C. Giving our lives as a living sacrifice is the greatest act of worship any of us can offer God.

Romans 12:1 says that surrendering our lives as a living sacrifice is our true and proper worship. It is the greatest form of worship that we can offer God. God is much more interested in us laying down our lives than He is in whether or not we sing like angels in church on Sunday. God is not impressed with my singing if my life is not being offered to him as a living sacrifice. It is our spiritual worship, it is the greatest act of worship.

Paul goes on to say that it will be holy and acceptable to God. What does holy mean? Does it mean perfect? No, holy literally means "set apart." When we make a decision to set ourselves apart to God, we are viewed by God as holy. Does that mean we are perfect? Absolutely not. But we are set apart. We are different! I'm listening and marching to the beat of a different drum. This is our true and proper worship!

Once we have offered our lives as a living sacrifice Paul gives us the second great key to living a surrendered life:

2. We must be transformed by the renewing of our minds.

The dedication of our lives begins at the altar but the transformation of our lives begins in our minds. The offering of our lives as living sacrifices is not a destination; it's the starting point! The moment of surrender is our starting point, the very beginning of a deeper spiritual walk with God.

#gone

"Romans is the profoundest piece of writing in existence."[3]

Samuel Taylor Coleridge

#biblesays

"Don't become so well-adjusted to your culture that you fit into it without even thinking. Instead, fix your attention on God. You'll be changed from the inside out. Readily recognize what he wants from you, and quickly respond to it. Unlike the culture around you, always dragging you down to its level of immaturity, God brings the best out of you, develops well-formed maturity in you."

romans chapter twelve verse two
the message

Once we have dedicated and laid down our lives, we still need to change. And here is the key: "Do not conform to the pattern of this world, but be transformed by the renewing of your mind."

The Greek word for "transformed" is "Metamorphoo". This is the root of our English word, "metamorphosis." "Meta" means "change." "Morphoo" means "form." A change of form takes place in order for the transformation of the caterpillar to become a butterfly. We need a metamorphosis in our lives, in our "everyday, ordinary life — our sleeping, eating, going-to-work, and walking-around life" before we can bear the kind of fruit that Paul talks about in the remainder of Romans 12.

It is interesting in the exposition of those two Greek words there is this sense that comes through the Greek of "changing form, in keeping with inner reality." Think about that for a moment. What God wants to happen is a changing of form in keeping with our inner reality. What is the inner reality? The inner reality is that once we accept Christ our inner nature changes; our inner reality changes. We become a new creation. The Bible calls us saints! Not because of our behavior, but because of our position. The Bible says I am justified by faith because of what Jesus did. My inner reality is that I am a saint, and I am holy! I'm looking pretty good on the inside, aren't I? I'm a saint, I'm holy, I'm a child of God, I'm set apart. What's my outer reality? We probably wouldn't want to see each other's worst moments from the past day or past week. The reality is that we are all flawed; we are all imperfect. The reality is we are all on a journey, we are all growing, and we all need to change.

What God is telling us through His Word is that we need to have a change in form on the outside that is in keeping with our inner reality. This is what Paul is talking about when he tells us we will be changed from the inside out, so that what's happening on the inside begins to be reflected in the outside. Change your mind, change your life. When we transform our mind, we will transform our life.

#biblesays

"As a man thinks so is he."

proverbs chapter twenty-three verse seven
new international version

There's an amazing story in the Gospels where Jesus takes Peter, James, and John up onto a mountain. The Bible says that Jesus was transfigured in front of them. That mountain became known as the Mount of Transfiguration, and Jesus literally was transfigured there. Matthew 17:2 says, "… and He was transfigured before them. His face shone like the sun and His clothes became as white as the light."

"Metamorphoo" is the word used in this passage for "transfiguration", and it literally means that his outward appearance was changed, reflecting His inner reality. This is an awesome picture of Jesus. Prior to this, His inner reality could only be seen partially, through His life, through His teaching and miracles, and through His character, but now there was a greater expression of His being as He was transfigured before the disciples. There was a change of form in keeping with His inner reality.

Consecration must be followed by transformation. There must be a change in our character. Paul goes on to tell us how we can be transformed. "Be transformed," he says, "by the renewing of your minds." Until we change the way we think, we will never be able to be transformed, and we will never change. Consecration must be followed by renewal. After we lay down our lives, we must then align our lives with God's Word. The reality is that until I begin to align my life with God's Word, I can never see all that Paul is talking about realized in my own life and in my own experience.

Our minds need to be renewed so that we are no longer conformed to the pattern of this world. Every one of us needs a new pattern of thinking if we want to have a new pattern of living. Where our mind goes, we will follow. Out of the abundance of the mind the life speaks. The shape of our thinking defines the shape of our lives, and the pattern of our thoughts defines the pattern of our lives. Paul says in Romans 12:2 [The Message], "Don't become so well-adjusted to your culture that you fit into it without even thinking. Instead, fix your attention on God. You'll be changed from the inside out."

#gone

"How many of God's children, although hitherto saved and possessed of a new life, still carry about them an old head. Nothing of their former theories, thought processes, or prejudices has been altered: only a Christian casing has been added."[4]

Watchman Nee

If we change the thought patterns that have shaped our life and replace them with new patterns of thinking from God's word, those new thoughts will actually create new neurological pathways in our brain. Paul is saying "Don't let the world shape the way you think; let God's Word shape the way you think, and you will find God's perfect shape for your life." The end of this verse says, "Then you will be able to test and approve what God's will is—his good, pleasing and perfect will." This is what Paul is saying: if you will lay your life on the altar, if you will align your life with God's Word, then you will know the creative power of God's word at work in your life.

One of the most significant things in my growth as a Christian was when Billy Graham came to town 1978, and I was signed up to be a counselor. It was the same crusade where my wife Di was saved, and I probably watched her walking down to the front with thousands of others to give their lives to the Lord. As a counselor at the crusade, I received some training on how to counsel people who came forward to give their lives to Jesus. One of the lessons involved in the training was to give us Scriptures cards to memorize.

I'm so thankful for that experience because it created a pattern for me, where I would write scriptures on little cards, and I'd memorize them every single day. At that time, I was working in a job that was not mentally challenging. I was working for a fabric importer in their warehouse measuring and rolling expensive velvets and damasks.

I would pull those little cards out, memorize the scriptures, put them away and then pull them out again. I eventually got to the point where I could quote scripture for hours non-stop, by memory. What was happening was that I was being transformed by the renewing of my mind. That's exactly what Paul is talking about.

Make a decision as an act of your will.

Don't conform but be transformed.

Surrender your life to the greatest adventure of all.

GONE.

#gone

"Don't let the world around you squeeze you into its own mold, but let God re-mold your minds from within."[5]

J.B. Phillips

#anonymous

Jesus' hidden years ... and yours

"I leave you then with a short story that came to me years ago about a young boy obviously destined for greatness.

>Whenever I am disappointed with my spot in life, I stop to think about the little boy who was trying out for a part in a school play. His mother told me that he'd set his heart on being in it, though she feared he would not be chosen. On the day the parts were awarded, I went with her to collect him after school. The boy rushed up to her, eyes shining with pride and excitement. "Guess what, Mom," he shouted, and then said those words that will remain a lesson to me: "I have been chosen to clap and cheer."

When we have been chosen to clap and cheer, may God find our spirits as sweet. Sweetness through hiddenness guarantees abundance in harvest in God's good and perfect time."[6]

Alicia Britt Chole
Anonymous

#gone

Turn Your Eyes Upon Jesus

"Turn your eyes upon Jesus. Look full in His wonderful face. And the things of earth with grow strangely dim. In the light of His glory and grace."[7]

Helen H. Lemmel

end notes

1. Matthew Henry, "Proverbs 31", Matthew Henry's Concise Commentary on the Bible, [Public Domain]
2. Alicia Britt Chole, Anonymous [Nashville, TN: Thomas Nelson, 2006], pg.3

THE BEGINNING | INTRODUCTION
1.David Bayliss. "Romans 12." Bible Exposition: http: //www.dabhand.org/Essays/Romans%2012%20%20The%20Second%20Road.htm. Last accessed September 21, 2013.
2. Alicia Britt Chole, Anonymous [Nashville, TN: Thomas Nelson, 2006], pg.5
MY OLD LIFE | BURNOUT
1. Ulrich Kraft, "Burned Out", Scientific American Mind, June/July 2006 pp. 28-33
2. Sir Winston Churchill, Speech, House of Commons, August 20, 1940.

MY NEW LIFE
CHAPTER ONE | EVERYDAY
1. Author Unknown
2. C. S. Lewis. BrainyQuote.com, Xplore Inc, 2013. http://www.brainyquote.com/quotes/quotes/c/cslewis119176.html, last accessed September 25, 2013.
3. Charles R Swindoll, Improving your Serve, [Waco: Word], 1981
4. John C. Maxwell, Today Matters: 12 Daily Practices to Guarantee Tomorrow's Success, [Claremont, FL: Paw Prints, 2008]
5. Basil S. Walsh, http://thinkexist.com/quotation/if_you_dont_know_where_you_are_going-how_can_you/199552.html, last accessed September 25, 2013
6. Diana Scharf-Hunt & Pam Hait, Studying smart: time management for college students, [HarperCollins, 1990]
7. Robert Puller, http://thinkexist.com/quotation/good_habits-once_established_are_just_as_hard_to/192688.html. Last accessed September 25, 2013.
8. Aristotle, BrainyQuote.com, Xplore Inc, 2013. http://www.brainyquote.com/quotes/quotes/a/aristotle145967.html. Last accessed September 25, 2013.
9. Rebecca Ruter Springer, My Dream of Heaven: A Nineteenth Century Spiritual Classic [Harrison House Publishers, 2009] pg. 21
10. Alicia Britt Chole, Anonymous [Nashville, TN: Thomas Nelson, 2006], pg.10

CHAPTER TWO | ORDINARY

1. Rainer Maria Rilke, Letters to a Young Poet: The Possibility of Being, [Penguin, 2013], pg.18

2. Matthew Henry, Thomas Scott, A Commentary upon the Holy Bible: Romans to Revelation, Volume 6, [London, The Religious Tract Society, 1835]. pg. 83

3. Matthew Henry, An Exposition of All the Books of the Old and New Testaments, Volume 4, [Barrington & Haswell, 1828] Pg. 56

4. C.S. Lewis, The Weight of Glory, [New York, NY: HarperCollins, 2001]

5. Amplified Bible, Romans 12:2, [The Lockman Foundation, 1987]

6. Matthew Henry, "Genesis 1", Matthew Henry's Concise Commentary on the Bible, [Public Domain]

7. Matthew Henry, "John 21", Matthew Henry's Concise Commentary on the Bible, [Public Domain]

8. Alicia Britt Chole, Anonymous, [Nashville, TN: Thomas Nelson, 2006], pg.27

CHAPTER THREE | SLEEPING

1. Victor Hugo, The Letters of Victor Hugo: From Exile, And After the Fall of the Empire, Volume 2 [Boston & NY, Houghton, Mifflin and Co, 1898], pg. 23

2. Mark Twain. BrainyQuote.com, Xplore Inc, 2013. http://www.brainyquote.com/quotes/quotes/m/marktwain108600.html, last accessed September 25, 2013.

3. Corrie Ten Boom, Clippings from My Notebook, Publication date: June 1982

4. Compiled by Pam Robertson, Pocket Graces, "General Graces, Rebecca J. Weston, c. 1890" [Church House Publishing, 2004], pg. 6

5. Alicia Britt Chole, Anonymous [Nashville, TN: Thomas Nelson, 2006], pg.30, 31

CHAPTER FOUR | EATING

1. Saint Thomas Aquinas. "Second Part of the Second Part Question 148" Article 1. Summa

2. Saint Thomas Aquinas. "Second Part of the Second Part Question 148" Article 4. Summa

3. Elizabeth Medes, "Americans Spend $151 a Week on Food; the High-Income, $180" http://www.gallup.com/poll/156416/americans-spend-151-week-food-high-income-180.aspx. Last accessed September 21, 2013

4. Natural Resources Defense Council, "Wasted: How America Is Losing Up to 40 Percent of Its Food from Farm to Fork to Landfill" http://www.nrdc.org/food/wasted-food.asp Last accessed September 21, 2013

5. ABC News Staff, "100 Million Dieters" http://abcnews.go.com/Health/100-million-dieters-20-billion-weight-loss-industry/story?id=16297197#.UVTcGBmMXk0 Last accessed September 21, 2013

6. Carrie Gann, "Fat Forecast"
http://abcnews.go.com/blogs/health/2012/05/07/fat-forecast-42-of-americans-obese-by-2030/ Last accessed September 21, 2013
7. Salynn Boyles, Louise Chang "How Many Calories Should I Eat Today"
http://www.webmd.com/food-recipes/news/20060505/how-many-calories-should-i-eat-today Last accessed September 21, 2013
8. USDA, "Weight Management and Calories"
http://www.choosemyplate.gov/weight-management-calories/resources.html
Last accessed September 21, 2013
9 David Schlundt, PhD, "Is there any Magic?"
http://healthpsych.psy.vanderbilt.edu/HealthPsych/weightfacts.htm
Last accessed September 21, 2013
10. Orson Welles. BrainyQuote.com, Xplore Inc, 2013.
http://www.brainyquote.com/quotes/quotes/o/orsonwelle100326.html, accessed
September 21, 2013.
11. CalorieKing, "Food Search" http://www.calorieking.com/foods/ Last accessed,
September 21, 2013
12. Alicia Britt Chole, Anonymous [Nashville, TN: Thomas Nelson, 2006], pg.69

CHAPTER FIVE | GOING TO WORK

1. Martin Luther: quoted in Leland Ryker, Work and Leisure in Christian Perspective.
[Portland, OR: Multnomah, 1987], pg. 130
2. Norman Marks, Sustainable Business Forum on 'Disturbing Survey on Business
Ethics', April 2012, http://sustainablebusinessforum.com/norman-marks/57229/disturbing-survey-business-ethics. Last accessed September 21, 2013.
3. Billy Graham, Message to the Chinese. International Herald Tribune [Paris, April 18,
1988], Columbia World of Quotations. Columbia University Press,1996.
4. A. W. Tozer, Gems from Tozer [Camp Hill, PA: WingSpread, 1979]. pg.15.
5. Saint Augustine. BrainyQuote.com, Xplore Inc, 2013.
http://www.brainyquote.com/quotes/quotes/s/saintaugus165165.html, last accessed
September 21, 2013.
6. Helen Keller, "The World I Live In and Optimism: A Collection of Essays", [Mineola,
NY, Courier Dover Publications, 2012], pg. 90
7. Brother Lawrence, "The Brother Lawrence Collection: Practice and Presence of God,
Spiritual Maxims, the Life of Brother Lawrence" [Radford, VA, Wilder Publications,
2008], pg. 31
8. C.S. Lewis, Weight of Glory [New York: HarperCollins, 2009], pg. 38.
9. Alicia Britt Chole, Anonymous [Nashville, TN: Thomas Nelson, 2006], pg.72

CHAPTER SIX | WALKING AROUND LIFE

1. Samuel Johnson, The works of Samuel Johnson, Volume 6 [London 1823] pg. 153

2. Benjamin Franklin. BrainyQuote.com, Xplore Inc, 2013.
http://www.brainyquote.com/quotes/quotes/b/benjaminfr125394.html, Last accessed October 1, 2013.
3. Mahatma Gandhi. BrainyQuote.com, Xplore Inc, 2013.
http://www.brainyquote.com/quotes/quotes/m/mahatmagan134953.html Last accessed September 24, 2013.
4. Henry Blackaby, Richard Blackaby, Claude King, Experiencing God: Knowing and Doing the Will of God [Nashville, TN: B&H Publishing Group, 2008] pg. 148
5. Alicia Britt Chole, Anonymous [Nashville, TN: Thomas Nelson, 2006], pg.87

CHAPTER SEVEN | PLACE IT

1. First known publication of the prayer of Saint Francis was in French magazine called La Clochette in 1912.
2. Dr. Kristie Leong, Can Rearranging Furniture be Obsessive-Compulsive Disorder?
http://www.healthguideinfo.com/living-with-ocd/p94359/ Last accessed September 24, 2013
3. A. B. Simpson, as quoted in Evangelism, A Biblical Approach, M. Cocoris, [Chicago, IL: Moody, 1984], pg. 29
4. John Newton, Amazing Grace, First published 1779, Public Domain
5. A.W. Tozer, Signposts. Christianity Today, v. 39, n. 13.

MY NOW LIFE | THE MEANTIME

1. Earl Nightingale. BrainyQuote.com, Xplore Inc, 2013.
http://www.brainyquote.com/quotes/quotes/e/earlnighti107070.html. Last accessed: September 24, 2013.
2. Alicia Britt Chole, Anonymous [Nashville, TN: Thomas Nelson, 2006], pg.101

THE END

1. Braveheart [1995]
2. Matthew Henry, Matthew Henry's Concise Commentary on the Bible, [Public Domain], Ephesians 6:19-24.
3. Matthew Henry, Matthew Henry's Concise Commentary on the Bible, [Public Domain], Ephesians 6:19-24.
4. Matthew Henry, Matthew Henry's Concise Commentary on the Bible, [Public Domain], Ephesians 6:19-24
5. Matthew Henry, Matthew Henry's Concise Commentary on the Bible, [Public Domain], Ephesians 6:19-24.
6. Matthew Henry, Matthew Henry's Concise Commentary on the Bible, [Public Domain], Ephesians 6:19-24.
7. Matthew Henry, Matthew Henry's Concise Commentary on the Bible, [Public Domain], Ephesians 6:19-24.

8. Matthew Henry, Matthew Henry's Concise Commentary on the Bible, [Public Domain], Ephesians 6:19-24.

9. Matthew Henry, Matthew Henry's Concise Commentary on the Bible, [Public Domain], Ephesians 6:19-24.

10. Alicia Britt Chole, Anonymous [Nashville, TN: Thomas Nelson, 2006], pg.160

IN ADDITION | ROMANS THEOLOGY

1. Martin Luther: Cited by David N. Steele and Curtis C. Thomas, Romans: An Interpretive Outline [Phillipsburg, New Jersey: Presbyterian and Reformed Publishing Company], pg. 1

2. Everett F. Harrison: Expositor's Bible Commentary, ed. by Frank Gaebelein [Grand Rapids, MI: Zondervan],10:127

3. Samuel Taylor Coleridge: Martyn Lloyd-Jones, Romans: The Gospel of God [Grand Rapids: MI, Zondervan], pp. 5-7

4. Watchman Nee: The Spiritual Man VOL.III [Anaheim, CA, Living Stream Ministry], Part 8, Chapter 3

5. J. B. Phillips, "The New Testament in Modern English", Romans 12:2, [HarperCollins, 1962].

6. Alicia Britt Chole, Anonymous [Nashville, TN: Thomas Nelson, 2006], pg.181

7. Helen H. Lemmel, Turn your eyes upon Jesus, [Public Domain, 1922]